BARRON'S BOOK NOTES

WILLIAM SHAKESPEARE'S

Henry IV, Part 1

BY

Andrea Kantor

SERIES EDITOR

Michael Spring
Editor, *Literary Cavalcade*
Scholastic Inc.

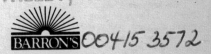

BARRON'S EDUCATIONAL SERIES, INC.
Woodbury, New York / London / Toronto / Sydney

ACKNOWLEDGMENTS

We would like to thank Loreto Todd, Senior Lecturer in English, University of Leeds, England, for preparing the chapter on Elizabethan English in this book.

We would like to acknowledge the many painstaking hours of work Holly Hughes and Thomas F. Hirsch have devoted to making the *Book Notes* series a success.

All inquiries should be addressed to:
Barron's Educational Series, Inc.
113 Crossways Park Drive
Woodbury, New York 11797

Library of Congress Catalog Card No. 84-18442

International Standard Book No. 0-8120-3419-8

Library of Congress Cataloging in Publication Data
Kantor, Andrea.
    William Shakespeare's Henry IV, part 1.

    (Barron's book notes)
    Bibliography: p. 108
    Summary: A guide to reading "Henry IV, Part 1"
With a critical and appreciative mind encouraging
analysis of plot, style, form, and structure. Also
includes background on the author's life and times,
sample tests, term paper suggestions, and a reading
list.
    1. Shakespeare, William, 1564–1616. King Henry IV.
Part 1.   2. Henry IV, King of England, 1367–1413,
in fiction, drama, poetry, etc. [1. Shakespeare,
William, 1564–1616. King Henry IV. Part 1. 2. English
literature—History and criticism] I. Title. II. Title:
Henry the Fourth, part one. III. Series.
PR2810.K36 1984   822.3'3   84-18442
ISBN 0-8120-3419-8 (pbk.)

PRINTED IN THE UNITED STATES OF AMERICA

456   550   98765432

CONTENTS

ADVISORY BOARD

HOW TO USE THIS BOOK

You have to know how to approach literature in order to get the most out of it. This *Barron's Book Notes* volume follows a plan based on methods used by some of the best students to read a work of literature.

Begin with the guide's section on the author's life and times. As you read, try to form a clear picture of the author's personality, circumstances, and motives for writing the work. This background usually will make it easier for you to hear the author's tone of voice, and follow where the author is heading.

Then go over the rest of the introductory material—such sections as those on the plot, characters, setting, themes, and style of the work. Underline, or write down in your notebook, particular things to watch for, such as contrasts between characters and repeated literary devices. At this point, you may want to develop a system of symbols to use in marking your text as you read. (Of course, you should only mark up a book you own, not one that belongs to another person or a school.) Perhaps you will want to use a different letter for each character's name, a different number for each major theme of the book, a different color for each important symbol or literary device. Be prepared to mark up the pages of your book as you read. Put your marks in the margins so you can find them again easily.

Now comes the moment you've been waiting for—the time to start reading the work of literature. You may want to put aside your *Barron's Book Notes* volume until you've read the work all the way through. Or you may want to alternate, reading the *Book Notes* analysis of each section as soon as you have finished reading the corresponding part of the original. Before you move on, reread crucial passages you don't fully understand. (Don't take this guide's analysis for granted—make up your own mind as to what the work means.)

Once you've finished the whole work of literature, you may want to review it right away, so you can firm up your ideas about what it means. You may want to leaf through the book concentrating on passages you marked in reference to one character or one theme. This is also a good time to reread the *Book Notes* introductory material, which pulls together insights on specific topics.

When it comes time to prepare for a test or to write a paper, you'll already have formed ideas about the work. You'll be able to go back through it, refreshing your memory as to the author's exact words and perspective, so that you can support your opinions with evidence drawn straight from the work. Patterns will emerge, and ideas will fall into place; your essay question or term paper will almost write itself. Give yourself a dry run with one of the sample tests in the guide. These tests present both multiple-choice and essay questions. An accompanying section gives answers to the multiple-choice questions as well as suggestions for writing the essays. If you have to select a term paper topic, you may choose one from the list of suggestions in this book. This guide also provides you with a reading list, to help you when you start research for a term paper, and a selection of provocative comments by critics, to spark your thinking before you write.

THE AUTHOR AND HIS TIMES

William Shakespeare was born into a tradesman's family in Stratford-upon-Avon in late April, 1564. When he was eighteen, Shakespeare married Anne Hathaway, ten years older than he. The young couple had a baby girl named Susanna six months later on May 26, 1583. In 1585 the birth of fraternal twins, Hamnet and Judith, completed the new family. But shortly afterward, Shakespeare left Stratford and moved to London, leaving his family behind.

No one knows what Shakespeare did for a living before he arrived in London. We do know that Shakespeare established himself in the London theater by 1592. He had become both an actor and a playwright with London's most prestigious theatrical troupe, the Lord Chamberlain's Men, headquartered in the first professional theater building built since the fall of the Roman Empire. It was called, simply, The Theater.

Open to the sky, The Theater had a large platform stage bounded on three sides by the audience. The stage was large (over thirty feet across), and was divided into upper and lower acting levels. Entrances and exits were made through two or three doors at the rear of the platform, into the "tiring house" where costumes were changed and speeches rehearsed. Scenery was kept at a bare minimum—a table and two benches might suggest a scene indoors or a tree represent a whole forest. The actors wore splendid costumes, however, and the acting style would have been broad and lively. Teenage boys played the women's parts. A gallery of musicians accompanied the actors, and the sound of battle was reproduced with effects backstage.

The audience would have been a cross-section of Londoners. Unruly apprentices stood on the ground around the stage, while merchants, fashionable women, and courtiers sat in three tiers of seats.

In the palaces along the River Thames Queen Elizabeth I ruled England amid a magnificent court. In an age when monarchs held absolute power, England was lucky to have such a queen. Elizabeth was a brilliant, outspoken, strong-willed woman, and a crafty politician who loved her country. Elizabeth I's reign was long (1558–1603) and dynamic, if not always peaceful. England had recently—under the reign of her sister, Queen Mary ("Bloody Mary")—been a Catholic country. Now it was Protestant and Puritan. But Elizabeth still had many Catholic enemies, such as northern England's powerful lords, and her cousin Queen Mary of Scotland. In 1569 the northern lords had rebelled against Elizabeth. They were defeated, but in the following year the Duke of Norfolk unsuccessfully attempted a coup to depose Elizabeth and place her Catholic cousin on the throne.

Although these rebellions failed, they worried Elizabeth; thereafter her subjects were required to listen to sermons on civil disobedience three times a year. The sermons followed a strict doctrine that the monarch was God's deputy on earth, and no subject had a right to oppose her. Rebellion against the monarch was rebellion against God, a terribly grave sin, to be punished by chaos on earth and eternal damnation for the rebels.

In 1588, King Philip II of Spain had sent the Armada, a huge flotilla of warships, to invade England. Elizabeth sent her navy to attack Philip's fleet, and after a week of merciless fighting the Armada was roundly defeated. Elizabeth's subjects rejoiced, and celebrated their country's greatness with an unprecedented patriotic fervor. One product of this burst of nationalist pride was the history play, which celebrated England's past and, like the sermons, instructed audiences in good civil behavior. Henry IV, Part 1 is one of ten plays Shakespeare wrote to celebrate England's history.

Shakespeare died in Stratford on April 23, 1616. He left no male heirs to continue his name. His only son, Hamnet, had died at age eleven. Susanna and Judith both married, but Susanna's only child Elizabeth was Shakespeare's last direct descendant. She died childless in 1670.

But Shakespeare left another kind of heir—thirty-seven plays and three major poems. In 1623, seven years after his death, two of Shakespeare's former colleagues in the theater published thirty-six of his plays, eighteen of them for the first time. We refer to this as the First Folio." In a prefatory poem, Ben Jonson praised his old friend and rival playwright as "the wonder of our stage." That verdict has stood through the centuries.

THE PLAY

The Plot

ACT I

King Henry IV is holding a political conference with his advisory council. His preparations for a holy crusade must be postponed because England's borders are threatened. The English general Mortimer was taken prisoner by Glendower after losing a battle in Wales, and another English lord, Hotspur, who has just won a battle in the north against the Scottish leader Douglas, refuses to send the king the prisoners he captured. King Henry is angry with Hotspur, and summons him to court.

Prince Hal, who should be helping his father King Henry govern the country, is somewhere in London roistering with an old friend, the disreputable Sir John Falstaff. A young thief named Poins meets them, and arranges with Falstaff to commit a highway robbery at Gad's Hill. Hal refuses to join them, until Poins privately tempts Hal with a plan to play a practical joke on Falstaff, which will show him up as a coward.

In the palace Hotspur, Northumberland, and Worcester argue with King Henry. The Percies, powerful northern lords, then plot to rebel against Henry, with whom they rebelled two years ago against King Richard II. They intend to enlist Henry's enemies (Glendower, Mortimer, Douglas, and the Archbishop of York) to help them overthrow the king.

ACT II

Two carriers discuss the condition of England and Gadshill (a member of Poins' gang) finds out when several rich merchants will be passing Gad's Hill on their way to London.

Falstaff and the band of thieves meet with Hal and Poins at Gad's Hill. Falstaff and the thieves rob the passing merchants; then Hal and Poins (in disguise) steal the stolen money. Falstaff defends himself briefly and unsuccessfully. Hal and Poins take the stolen money to London.

Meanwhile at Warkworth Castle in the north, Hotspur receives a letter from a lord who refuses to join the rebellion conspiracy. He rides off to meet the rebel leaders in Wales.

In a London tavern Hal and Poins are waiting for Falstaff to arrive. Falstaff and the thieves burst into the tavern, and tell an exaggerated story about their encounter with an army of thieves at Gad's Hill. Hal exposes Falstaff as a liar. Then news of the Percy rebellion reaches the tavern. Hal, who's been summoned to court, prepares for his father's inevitable scolding by rehearsing with Falstaff the meeting with Henry. At the height of their play-acted argument, a sheriff arrives to arrest Falstaff for theft. Falstaff hides, and Hal lies to protect him from criminal punishment. Falstaff falls asleep, and Hal picks his pocket before returning to court.

ACT III

In a castle in Wales the rebels meet to divide the leadership of England into three parts. Glendower and Hotspur quarrel, but peace settles among the rebels while they say good-bye to their wives. They ride to Shrewsbury, where the battle against Henry will shortly take place.

In the palace Henry accuses Hal of wasting his youth and disappointing his family. Henry compares Hal unfavorably with King Richard II and with Hotspur. Hal promises to turn over a new leaf, and vows to gain honor equal to Hotspur's by fighting a glorious battle. Father and son are reconciled, and Henry gives his son command of one-third of the royal army.

In the tavern Falstaff quarrels with the hostess over who picked his pocket. Hal arrives dressed for battle, and settles the dispute by admitting he did it. Hal gives Falstaff command over a troop of foot soldiers, and returns to court to help with battle preparations. Falstaff plots ways of turning the war to his personal profit.

ACT IV

Hotspur, Worcester, and Douglas are camped at Shrewsbury, waiting for the rest of their allies. Messengers arrive with news that Northumberland and Glendower won't be joining them in battle. Hotspur and Douglas resolve to carry out their plans anyway, despite their greatly reduced forces. Hearing that Prince Hal is leading a gloriously attired army toward Shrewsbury, Hotspur swears to kill him in single combat.

Falstaff marches his foot soldiers toward the battlefield. Their raggedy appearance shocks Hal, but Falstaff lectures him on the realities of war.

Sir Walter Blunt arrives at the rebel camp with an offer of pardon from Henry. Hotspur airs his grievances against Henry, and sends Blunt back to the royal camp without an answer.

At York, the archbishop is very worried because the king's army outnumbers the rebels three to one.

ACT V

Worcester and Henry try to reach a peaceful settle-ment, and Hal intervenes to offer himself in single combat to Hotspur, in place of a full-scale battle. Henry forbids this, and sends Worcester back to the rebel camp with an ultimatum.

Worcester lies to Hotspur about Henry's peace offer, and the battle challenge is given. During the battle Henry fights Douglas, and Hal fights Hotspur. Hal rescues Henry from Douglas, and kills Hotspur. Falstaff, meanwhile, leads his soldiers into the thick-est fighting, yet he debunks honor, and pretends to fall down dead when challenged by Douglas. Stand-ing between the bodies of Hotspur, his greatest rival, and Falstaff, his best friend, Hal praises Hotspur and teases Falstaff, then walks away. Falstaff jumps up and defends his seemingly cowardly behavior. Hal returns, amazed to find Falstaff still alive. Hal allows Falstaff to take credit for killing Hotspur, a lie on which Falstaff stakes his future reputation.

The king's army wins the battle. Henry orders the executions of the rebel prisoners, but Hal insists on freeing Douglas. Henry divides the royal army, proudly giving his son command of one-half. The two halves split to the north and west, marching away to fight the remaining rebel leaders.

The Characters

King Henry IV

In order to understand what is troubling King Henry, you should be familiar with the events sur-rounding the deposition of Richard, and Henry's rise to power.

These events will be described four times in *Henry IV, Part 1*: by Henry, by Hotspur (twice), and by Worcester. Each account of how and why Henry became king differs, just as newspapers or history books today often disagree about a single event.

Shakespeare never makes Henry's motives entirely clear, and Henry is relatively quiet about them. You don't know if Henry rose to the throne on a tide of popular opinion that he never anticipated when he returned from exile, or if he carefully planned the entire "election," and always meant to steal the crown from his cousin Richard.

Because Henry's motives aren't clear, you could form two perfectly feasible, but entirely different, portraits of Henry. You can see him as Hotspur does: as a "vile politician" who calculated every move up the ladder of success, and manipulated his friends and his country into making him king. Or you can see Henry as the beneficiary of irresistible political forces: a good politician who knew how to take advantage of opportunity and who understood how to use power most effectively.

Even though Henry is a usurper, he wants to unite his kingdom and uphold her laws. He may not be a legal king, but he's a better ruler than Richard.

Prince Hal

Hal is the Prince of Wales, Henry's son and heir. When Henry dies Hal will inherit the crown, and rule England as King Henry V. But to his father, Hal doesn't seem like much of an heir. Instead of living at court and helping his father govern England, Hal carouses in the taverns of Eastcheap with a band of drunkards and petty thieves.

Like his father, Hal wasn't born to be a king. When he was twelve, Henry usurped the throne from King Richard, and Hal suddenly found himself next in line to be king. Immediately after Henry's coronation Hal moved into the tavern world, to drink and joke with Falstaff, and to rob for fun. Hal tells you early on that he's only pretending to be dissolute, and intends to stage a stunning reformation of character that will make him look even better to the eyes of the unexpecting court. This may sound like an excuse, but when war breaks out Hal does leave the tavern world, and returns to the court to fight with his father against the Percies.

Whereas Henry never seems at ease anywhere, Hal is equally at home in court and tavern. At Shrewsbury he fights like a perfect knight, with great courage and magnanimity. In the tavern he mingles easily with the commoners, and even the lowly waiters hail him as the "king of courtesy." As a nobleman aged about twenty, Hal has been trained in the arts of chivalry, good manners, and military skills. But he's still learning the art of being a prince. Some readers believe Hal goes to the tavern to escape his new serious responsibilities. Others think that he goes there to adjust to his new role, and learn something about the lives of the people he will one day have to govern.

Hal has inherited Henry's flair for politics, as his plan for a spectacular "reformation" shows. Unlike Henry, Hal will inherit an untainted crown. The combination of political skill and rightful claim will make Hal the perfect king.

Most readers judge Hal as a person, not as a king, and find him lacking on several counts. He's cold and detached from his companions, whom he vows to banish. He uses people for personal advantage, whether as part of his self-help course in kingship or for sheer amusement. He enjoys cruel practical jokes. Honor is a commodity to Hal, something he must win for his kingly image, not something he feels is necessary for leading a virtuous life. His favorite imagery is borrowed from the accounting profession. He counts men's attributes like coins in a change purse. His behavior toward people is capricious: One moment he promises them the earth, the next he cruelly upbraids them.

Other readers sympathize with Hal, recognizing that a prince is different from other men. We may value spontaneity and warmth in our friends, but we require sensible planning and a cool head in our leaders. When asked to join a highway robbery, Hal dispassionately weighs the pros and cons of the scheme before agreeing to participate. He learns about vice from Falstaff, but ultimately he rejects the criminal life as completely as he rejects Hotspur's wild romanticism. Hal seems more in control of himself than anyone else in this play. Every other character makes grand promises he doesn't keep. Hal promises to fight loyally for his father, and he does. He promises to win honor from Hotspur in battle, and he does. In a world given to lying and stealing, Hal proves he's no counterfeit, but a true prince of England.

Hotspur

Northumberland's son Hotspur is often seen as the romantic hero of this play. Many readers respond to him more than to the cool, enigmatic Hal. Even King Henry wishes Hotspur were his son. The very embodiment of military courage and virtue, Hotspur is a quick-tempered, energetic young man whose straightforward approach to life is both attractive and dangerous.

On one hand, Hotspur is a knight in shining armor whose reckless and passionate nature makes him more attractive than the calculating, hypocritical politicians who surround him.

Hotspur is completely dedicated to winning honor, but this blinds him to many realities. He values honor more than his own life. He's impatient with anyone who can't understand his devotion to an ideal of knightly behavior; he ridicules Hal's tavern life, and scoffs at Glendower's interest in magic. To Hotspur, anything less than winning honor is a waste of time. Politicians enrage him with their endless talk and compromises. He dreams of being the greatest knight on earth, and challenges anyone who claims to be his rival in battle.

Hotspur's thirst for battle is self-destructive; he pursues honor like an addict. He allows events to give him direction without stopping to think about the consequences of his actions. Once he's committed to a cause, nothing and no one can stand in his way. Northumberland despairs of Hotspur's rash nature, and fears his son might ruin their plans. He refuses to listen to good counsel, and his overconfidence blinds him to the guile or weakness of others. He may love his wife, but he doesn't trust her to keep quiet about the rebellion plans. At Shrewsbury he refuses to wait for reinforcements and dies a fanatic's death, as a pawn in Worcester's political game.

King Henry sees Hotspur as a model for Prince Hal. Henry sees himself in Hotspur—both are rebels against a king; both are ambitious and capable of leading great political revolutions. But both Henry and Hotspur fail to see their moral impostures. Falstaff and Hall alone see through Hotspur's glamorous facade: Hotspur's dead body is simply a warehouse of honor from which Falstaff can steal a good military reputation and Hal can steal the honor he requires for kingship.

Hotspur is called the "king of honor," but can a rebel and a traitor be a king? His own uncle Worcester accuses him of "apprehending a world of figures"; is this a man you'd want as a leader of real men? Hotspur may be heroic, but he's misguided by his family and too narrow in his thinking. He dashes off on a quest for military glory, and rushes his country into civil war because of a personal insult. In this play Shakespeare is trying to define what makes a good king. Hotspur may be an attractive person, but when we judge his leadership qualities, he falls short.

Falstaff

Sir John Falstaff, knight of the realm and stealer of purses, is an endless stream of contradictions. You can't sum him up in a capsule description; he seems to evade categorization as deftly as he evades Hal's verbal traps. He changes roles and moral postures as easily and as often as anyone else changes clothes.

He's old and young; fat and limber; cowardly and fearless; sinful and virtuous. Falstaff is a liar, a drunkard, and a thief—but he's a brilliant conversationalist, well educated in the Bible and classical and contemporary Elizabethan literature.

Although clothed in a mountain of fat, Falstaff seems to strip the world naked, and laughs at the court's pretensions about abstract ideals like honor and good government. He mocks all the serious pursuits in the play—honor, law and order, reasonableness, and justice. He even makes himself look ridiculous, and then asks you to agree that his view of the world is great fun.

Falstaff's name is a contraction of the words "false staff," which can mean a cracked or brittle cane, and a misleader. A false leader is a counterfeit king. Falstaff is King Henry's comical counterpart who distorts Henry's royal image like the trick mirrors in a carnival funhouse. Whereas Henry symbolizes authority and civil order, images of disorder cluster around Falstaff—anarchy, gluttony, and falseness surround the old knight like dancing figures of the Seven Deadly Sins.

Falstaff is also a substitute father for Hal. He preaches a kind of revolutionary politics to the young prince. Falstaff begs Hal to make thieves respectable, and to abolish capital punishment. He tries to tempt Hal into committing highway robbery. But Hal refuses to be corrupted by Falstaff's temptations. He calls Falstaff a "villainous abominable misleader of youth" and "that old white-bearded Satan." He banishes Falstaff and his reign of misrule.

Falstaff's view of life is realistic and hard. He sees that friends are disloyal and money is hard to come by. The reality of war is that men are killed. It's easier to sin than to pursue the pious virtues of a devout Christian. These opinions are cynical perhaps, but Falstaff tempers his harsh view of life with good-natured enthusiasm. When confronted with adversity, Falstaff understands that a good hearty laugh is healthier than crippling anxiety, such as that which plagues humorless King Henry.

Other Elements
SETTING

The setting for the play is England. There are seven scenes in London and seven scenes at Shrewsbury. There are also two scenes in Rochester and one each at York, Wales, and Warkworth Castle in Northumberland. As you can see from a map, the action covers almost the entire country. You also move through different kinds of social settings.

In London you spend time at the king's palace and in a tavern in Eastcheap. You pass along roads leading from Dover to London and from London to Shrewsbury by way of Coventry. You hear about Henry's landing at Ravenspur and his meeting with the Percies at Doncaster. You visit a hotel in Rochester and a mysterious castle in Wales. You hear about battles along the Scottish and Welsh borders.

England becomes more than a physical setting; it is almost like another character. You are shown how much her welfare depends on power and political wisdom. You are shown how important it is for a king-to-be to know all levels of life in England.

The time period of the play is the early fifteenth century—June 1402 to July 1403 to be exact—but the characters onstage really are drawn from the late sixteenth century—1596–97, when Shakespeare wrote the play. Each character has his own sense of time. Hotspur burns it, Falstaff wastes it, King Henry worries about its passing, and Prince Hal carefully counts and measures it. This elastic sense of time is matched by Shakespeare's flexible sense of historical time in drama; he compresses the events of one year into a timespan that seems to amount to no more than a few weeks. Some scenes, especially those at court, are tense and brisk; others, such as the tavern scenes, roll along easily, taking all the time in the world.

THEMES

Many themes run through *Henry IV, Part 1*. The following are some of the most important.

1. A STUDY OF HISTORY

Shakespeare is dramatizing an important and insecure period of English history, when King Henry IV's reign was plagued by civil rebellions, and Prince Hal's dissolute behavior brought the safety of the succession into question. In the 1590s Elizabeth, old and childless, was in danger of dying without an heir. If the wrong candidate was chosen, England was bound to erupt into civil war. Shakespeare turned to King Henry IV's time to examine the issue of authority and rebellion so crucial for his own age.

2. AUTHORITY AND REBELLION

In Shakespeare's time it was taken for granted that a king had absolute authority over his country. But if the king does not rule by hereditary right then political power becomes important—how to win it and how to use it. The question of how to maintain order also becomes crucial, because the king's authority may not be accepted by everyone. When treason threatens the court, all of England is thrown into doubt and confusion. The very harmony between man and nature seems to be affected, and brother fights brother in an endless struggle for power.

3. THE EDUCATION OF A PRINCE

As King Henry V, Hal will be called "the mirror of all Christian kings." Prince Hal's education in becoming the perfect king is portrayed in this play. He must steer a course between Hotspur's virtues and Falstaff's vices, and satisfy the double demands of royal authority and political power.

4. A PORTRAIT OF ENGLAND

Although the events of the play took place in 1403, the characters are modeled on Elizabethan men and women. You hear or see a cross-section of Shakespeare's own society: thieves, prostitutes, ballad-singers, innkeepers, scolding wives, apprentices, carriers, merchants, pilgrims, magicians, sheriffs, soldiers, lords, ladies, and royal princes. You see the Welsh and the Scots as well as the English. You learn about Elizabethan food and drink and their prices; you learn about Elizabethan political conferences, transportation, communications networks, military weapons, and plays. These all contribute to a rich and lively picture of Elizabethan daily life.

5. HONOR

The pursuit of honor is one of the characters' chief motivations. Hotspur seeks military glory and fame above all else, and recklessly gives up his life to save his honor. His courage is thrilling, but his single-mindedness blinds him to the weaknesses of others. Prince Hal seems to lack honor; he strays from court and robs for sport. He speaks of honor as a mere commodity. Yet he shows true honor later; he is valiant in battle and generous toward both friends and enemies. Falstaff, on the other hand, scoffs at honor itself. He prefers to live in sin rather than die for honor. But Falstaff doesn't scoff at the rewards of honor. Like Hotspur, he's ambitious to win titles and respect. Falstaff, who steals for a living, cheats to win honor at Shrewsbury. Yet, though his friends call him a coward, his brilliant wit and expansive view of humanity win him another kind of respect.

These different uses for honor lead you to wonder what honor's ultimate value really is. People talk a lot about it, but what place can honor have in a world ruled by a usurper, where a rebel is called the king of honor?

6. COUNTERFEITING

Trying to decide what's real or counterfeit, true or false, is one of the major concerns of the play. Characters ask each other, and you, to decide on the accuracy of news and reports, on different versions of history, and on the reality of a man's reputation.

The idea of counterfeiting is bound up in the king's usurpation of the crown—since his claim is dubious, all other claims for authenticity begin to be doubted. The idea is emphasized in the imagery of stolen and cracked crowns (both the coins and the symbol of kingship) that are passed off as being legal and legitimate.

7. FATHERS AND SONS

Throughout the ages fathers have wanted their sons to emulate them, and sons have displeased their fathers by showing independence of mind. Each son in this play has two fathers—one natural and one moral. Henry is Hal's natural father, and Falstaff is Hal's moral father. Whom shall Hal imitate? The false king or the thieving knight? Hotspur has two fathers—Northumberland, who scolds Hotspur's quick temper, and Worcester, who leads him into rebellion and lies to him to protect his own life. Whom should he follow? Should the sons imitate their fathers, or are they right to reject them as models and pursue their own courses of action, no matter what the consequences may be?

STYLE

The worlds of the court and the tavern speak in different styles: The court characters use stately verse, and the commoners in the tavern world use lively prose. Hal, because he spans both worlds, is the only character to speak in both styles.

Shakespeare's writing style manages to sound realistic in both poetry and prose. His characters sound like real people with vivid imaginations. Shakespeare varies the stresses and sound of the words and the length of sentences to create different kinds of verbal music, which gives you an illusion of real speech.

FORM AND STRUCTURE

The structure of the play is episodic; that is, scenes do not follow one line of action, but alternate from one set of characters to another. This allows two plots to develop at the same time, with connections and contrasts between them drawn continually. One plot concerns the Percies' rebellion against Henry; the second plot concerns Falstaff's life in the tavern with Prince Hal. The tavern scenes mirror the court scenes: Whatever happens in one plot, happens in the other but on a different scale.

Individual characters, too, are contrasted in pairs. Hotspur and Falstaff, Henry and Hal, Henry and Falstaff, Hal and Hotspur, Worcester and Falstaff, are the most important character contrasts. They parody each other and thus you can see how they see each other. Hal parodies Hotspur and Henry; Hotspur parodies Henry, Glendower, and the king's messenger; Falstaff parodies Henry and a host of other men.

SOURCES AND ROYAL LINEAGE

The outline of the historical events in the play may be found in Raphael Holinshed's 1587 edition of *The Chronicles of England, Scotland, and Ireland* (first published in 1577). This massive compilation of fact, legend, hearsay, and moralizing was a popular Elizabethan source for England's history from its beginnings to the middle of the sixteenth century. In his account

THE ROYAL LINEAGE OF HENRY IV

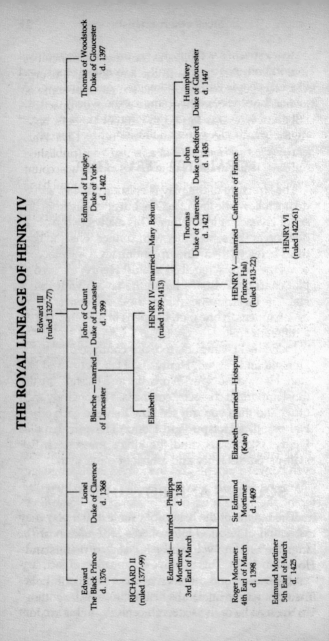

of Henry IV's reign, Holinshed stresses the difficulties Henry had trying to govern the kingdom as a usurper. Shakespeare rearranged the sequence of some of the incidents to give them more dramatic impact.

Shakespeare also turned to Samuel Daniel's epic-length poem, *The First Four Books of the Civil Wars Between the Two Houses of Lancaster and York* (published in 1595). Daniel unified Holinshed's rambling account of the Percy rebellion, emphasizing the immoral basis of King Henry's reign. Shakespeare followed Daniel in changing Hal's and Hotspur's ages so that both men are young. (The real Hal was 16 when Hotspur was 36.) Daniel also gave Shakespeare precedent for having Hal kill Hotspur at Shrewsbury. (There's no historical evidence that it happened that way.)

Stories about Prince Hal's wild youth began to circulate shortly after his death. An anonymous play called *The Famous Victories of King Henry V*, which was most likely written before 1588, was published in 1598. There Shakespeare probably found his models for Hal's tavern companions, the highway robbery, the tavern play, and Henry's concern over his dissolute son.

ELIZABETHAN ENGLISH

All languages change. Differences are apparent even between parents and their children. If language can change in only one generation, imagine how different the English used by Shakespeare some four hundred years ago will be from the English you use today. The following information on Shakespeare's language will make it easier for you to understand *Henry IV, Part 1*.

Adjectives, nouns, and verbs were less rigidly confined to grammatical roles in Shakespeare's day. Verbs could be used as adjectives, such as *christen*, for which you would today say "Christian," as in ". . . and can call them all by their christen names,/as Tom, Dick, and Francis" (II, iv, 7–8). Adjectives could be used as adverbs. In "Here is a dear, a true industrious friend" (I, i, 63), *true* means "truly" or "loyally." *Grievous* is used for "grievously" in "He cannot come, my lord, he is grievous sick" (IV, i, 17).

Wordplay often involved the use of a word from two parts of speech. For example, Falstaff uses *cold* as a verb meaning "trick," and *colt* meaning "horse" is used as a verb by Prince Hal:

> Falstaff: What a plague mean ye to colt me thus?
> Prince: Thou liest; thou art not colted, thou art uncolted.
> (II, ii, 37–39)

The meanings of words undergo changes; *chip* extended its meaning from a small piece of wood to a small piece of silicon, for example. Many of the words in Shakespeare still exist today, but their meanings have changed. The change may be small, as in the case of *suddenly* meaning "at once" or "immediately," in: "Well, I'll repent, and that suddenly, while I am in some liking . . ." (III, iii, 5–6). Or the change can be important. *Doubt* means "strongly suspect" or "fear," *starve* means "die," *trick* means "characteristic," *wanton* means "luxuriant," and *advertisement* means "information."

Words not only change their meanings, they are frequently discarded from the language altogether. In the past *leman* meant "sweetheart" and *sooth* meant "truth." The following are some of the words used in *Henry IV* that are no longer in current English (you can usually figure them out from their contexts):

minion *(I, i, 85):* darling
sack *(I, ii, 3):* wine
leaping houses *(I, ii, 9):* brothels
quiddities *(I, ii, 46):* quibbles
gib-cat *(I, ii, 76):* castrated tomcat
cozening *(I, ii, 114):* cheating
hardiment *(I, iii, 103):* valor, courage
corrival *(I, iii, 217):* associate, partner
bots *(II, i, 9):* intestinal worms
jordan *(II, i, 19):* chamberpot
franklin *(II, i, 54):* man with freehold land
squire *(II, ii, 13):* measure, measuring instrument
colt *(II, ii, 38):* trick
manage *(II, iii, 50):* horsemanship
hest *(II, iii, 63):* command
mammets *(II, iii, 97):* puppets
skinker *(II, iv, 24):* one who draws wine, bartender
netherstocks *(II, iv, 117):* stockings
bombast *(II, iv, 331):* cotton stuffing
bombard *(II, iv, 457):* wine vessel
cressets *(III, i, 16):* beacons
bootless *(III, i, 74):* unsuccessful
cates *(III, I, 175):* delicacies
bate *(III, iii, 2):* lose weight
ancients *(IV, ii, 24):* ensigns
owe *(V, ii, 77):* own

Shakespearean verb forms differ from modern usage in two main ways. Questions and negatives could be formed without using *do* or *did*, as when Hotspur asks his wife in Act II, Scene iii, line 100: "What sayest thou, Kate?" where today you would say: "What do you say, Kate?" In the same speech Hotspur tells her: "I love thee not;/I care not for thee, Kate" *(94–96)* where instead you would say: "I don't love you; I don't care for you."

A number of past participles and past tense forms that were used then are considered ungrammatical today. Among them are *holp* for "helped": ". . . which our own hands Have holp to make so portly" *(I, iii, 12–13); set* for "seated":

> Prince: Well, here I am set.
> Falstaff: And here I stand.
>
> *(II, iv, 444–445)*

and *forgot* for "forgotten": "If that the king/Have any way your good deserts forgot" *(IV, iii, 52–53)*.

Shakespeare and his contemporaries had the extra pronoun *thou*, which was used to address a person who was one's equal or social inferior. Frequently, a person in power used *thou* to a child or subordinate, but was addressed *you* in return. For example, in Act II, Scene iii, lines 78–79, when Lady Percy speaks to Hotspur:

> Lady Percy: But hear you, my lord.
> Hotspur: What sayest thou, my lady?

You was obligatory if more than one person was being addressed: "I know you all, and will awhile uphold/The unyoked humor of your idleness." *(I, ii, 200–201)*. It could also be used to indicate respect, as in Act I, Scene iii, line 24, when the Earl of Northumberland addresses the king: "Those prisoners in your Highness' name demanded. . . ."

There is one more pronominal reference that you should know about. King Henry uses the royal *we* to stress his sovereignty, as in "Then this remains, that we divide our power." *(V, v, 35)*.

Prepositions were less standardized in Elizabethan English than they are today. You'll find several uses in *Henry IV* that you would have to modify in your contemporary speech. Among them are *on* for "to," in "the victory fell on us"; *with* for "by," in "Thence to be wrenched with an unlineal hand"; *of* for "from," in "For of no right, nor color like to right"; and *on* for "of," in "enamored on his follies."

Contemporary English allows only one negative per statement. If you said, "I haven't none" you would be considered ungrammatical. But Shakespeare often used two or more negatives for emphasis, as in Act III, Scene i, line 127, when Glendower tells Hotspur: "No, nor you shall not" and in Act III, Scene iii, lines 115–117, when Falstaff tells the hostess: "There's no more faith in thee than in a stewed prune,/nor no more truth in thee than in a drawn fox."

Don't worry if all this seems confusing. Most of the language is clear as you read the play, and almost every edition includes a glossary.

The Story

ACT I

ACT I, SCENE I

In this scene at court you see King Henry's policies being frustrated and his authority snubbed; you witness his despair over Prince Hal and his admiration for Hotspur.

Lines 1–33

In the palace in London, King Henry meets with his lord counselors to discuss the current political crisis.

The country is obviously torn up by internal fighting for power. Henry describes this, feelingly, for his counselors. He wants to establish peace and order in the kingdom, to have his subjects "march all one way," but instead there's war and uncertainty. He explains that he is going to take the warring nobles on a crusade to the Holy Land, to stop them from fighting at home.

NOTE: Crusades were medieval religious wars fought by European Christians against Muslims in the Holy Land. The men who went on the crusades hoped to win salvation, honor, or riches during the long campaigns. By the sixteenth century crusades were also used by kings as a strategy to divert attention from domestic trouble, by focusing their subjects' attention on foreign problems.

The struggle to achieve his political aims is apparently wearing out Henry. He's "shaken" and "wan," anxious and tired when you first see him. Shakespeare doesn't tell you why the king is under such a great strain, but his original audience would already have known the causes of the civil uprisings as well as you know the causes of the American Civil War. King Henry IV is a usurper—a criminal, a thief who stole the crown. Henry and his supporters forced the rightful king of England, Richard II, to resign his crown only one year before this play begins. The civil rebellions may simply be a fight for political power, such as accompanies any change in leadership.

Shakespeare's audience would have believed that God is punishing Henry by bringing anarchy and rebellion to England. No matter how good a ruler Henry might be, only two things will bring peace to England: 1. Henry can pay for his sin by going on a crusade to Jerusalem; or 2. he can hold onto the crown long enough to pass it on to his son, Prince Hal. But

the domestic crisis in England is keeping him from
going to Jerusalem. Soon you will find out what the
problem is with his son.

NOTE: Throughout the play images of violence,
disorder, and disease will appear. They're signs that
Henry hasn't been forgiven yet. Shakespeare won't
let you forget Henry's unpaid-for crime.

Lines 34–62

Westmoreland, the king's chief counselor, steps
forward to report on a meeting that took place the
previous night. We were discussing the crusade,
Westmoreland says cautiously when a messenger
from the west suddenly burst into the room with
grave news: Lord Mortimer had lost a battle in Wales
against the "irregular and wild" Owen Glendower,
and Mortimer was taken prisoner.

Henry immediately cancels the crusade. Will it ever
take place? You will see his anxiety turn into frustra-
tion and then rage.

Westmoreland has even more unwelcome news:
another messenger had brought word that young
Harry Percy, "Hotspur," was fighting a bloody battle
in the north; its outcome was still unknown.

Lines 63–76

Henry gestures to a travel-stained lord, Sir Walter
Blunt, who has just brought the king an updated
report: Hotspur won the battle, taking several Scottish
lords prisoner. "And is not this an honorable spoil?/A
gallant prize?" Henry eagerly asks Westmoreland (obviously Henry admires Hotspur). Westmoreland
agrees that it's a victory worthy of a prince.

Lines 77–110

The news of Hotspur's victory then makes the king turn sad, because his own son wasn't there. Hotspur, Henry says, is "the theme of honor's tongue," while Prince Hal's reputation is stained with "riot and dishonor." Henry doesn't have only political rebellion to worry about—his own son rebels against him. Henry wishes Hotspur and Hal could exchange places, so that Hotspur would be the next king of England.

But Henry is as angry with Hotspur as he is proud of him. Hotspur disobeyed a direct order to send his prisoners to the king. He writes that he'll send Henry only one prisoner, who happens to be of royal blood. Westmoreland suggests that Hotspur's uncle Worcester may be responsible for this disobedience, because Worcester is "malevolent to you in all aspects."

Hotspur is, after all, behaving according to the law of arms, but Henry is reacting as though his authority has been flouted.

NOTE: The law of arms stated that the victor in a battle could keep all prisoners of war, except for prisoners of royal blood; these had to be sent to the king.

Henry impatiently dismisses his counselors, having ordered Hotspur to court to explain his behavior. This incident with the Scottish prisoners has now set up a conflict between King Henry and Hotspur's family, the Percies. Watch for it to flare up soon.

ACT I, SCENE II

In this scene set in Prince Hal's apartment in London, Falstaff and Hal talk about crime and punishment, and a robbery is planned. Remember, this is the world Hal comes to to escape from life in his father's court. You've heard about Hal's bad reputation; compare that with how he appears in person. You'll also now meet his favorite companion, Sir John Falstaff.

Lines 1–73

Many stage directors begin this scene with Falstaff asleep, snoring loudly, showing you a vivid emblem of sloth, the vice of idleness. How unlike our first glimpse of King Henry! The king was tired and anxious, but awake, making speeches and political decisions. The sleeping Falstaff, belly spilling over his belt, is the very image of good health and irresponsibility.

Hal wakes up Falstaff. "Now, Hal," the old knight bellows, "what time of day is it, lad?" The prince hoots with laughter. Why should you want to know the time, he asks Falstaff, when you spend all of it in a drunken oblivion, aroused only by more wine, women, and the chance of stealing more wallets?

NOTE: Look at the images of time in Scene 1— the sense of urgency, the racing messengers, the rapidly dated news bulletins. Time is a precious commodity at court. But now here's Falstaff, gloriously wasting time. This is just one of many ways he rejects the conventions of law and order.

Now thoroughly awakened by Hal's scolding, Falstaff daydreams about his lucky future, when his friend Prince Hal will be King Henry V of England. Falstaff cheerfully admits that, at present, he's a thief, with a bad reputation and even worse prospects—the gallows. (In Shakespeare's time the penalty for stealing was hanging.) "Will you make thieves respectable when you are king?" wonders Falstaff. Hal promises to raise Falstaff's social status—as high as the hangman's noose. "Do thou not," Falstaff begs, "when thou art King, hang a thief." Hal promises to make Falstaff his chief hangman.

Falstaff hopes Hal will behave on the throne of England the same way he behaves in the tavern. King Henry, you know, also thinks Hal will behave that way—that's why he's so worried about Hal. But maybe they're selling him short. Does Hal say anything in this scene that implies that he will disregard justice? Every time Falstaff asks him to allow criminals to escape punishment, Hal upholds English law, and intends to go on hanging thieves.

Falstaff never lets Hal forget that one day he will rule England. Phrases like "when thou art king" and "were it not here apparent that thou art heir apparent" must irritate Hal. They're reminders that Hal can't spend all his life in the tavern, unless he's willing to disregard the responsibilities of kingship. You've just seen how weighty his father's responsibilities are. Now Shakespeare makes you curious to see whether Hal will be able to bear the burden when his time comes.

Lines 74–107

Falstaff becomes depressed, convinced he can never escape hanging. He puts on a mock-religious attitude, acting like a Puritan, and solemnly promises to repent his evil ways. Hal, Falstaff announces sternly, you have corrupted me. Before I knew you, I was virtuous. But now I am wicked, and I must reform.

Throughout the play, whenever he becomes depressed Falstaff will look into his past and see only virtue and slenderness. He dislikes the present, with its fears and poverty. He's afraid of the gallows, of the hard realities of his life, and so he escapes into fantasy. He idealizes his own past.

Although Falstaff's claim that the young prince corrupted him is preposterous, Hal doesn't get angry. He cleverly uses Falstaff's own words to trap him. "Where shall we take a purse tomorrow?" Hal slyly suggests. Falstaff instantly leaps to the bait. The prince rocks with laughter: "I see a good amendment of life in thee," he cries, "from praying to purse-taking." Insulted, Falstaff defends himself. He argues that because thieving is his true calling in life, it isn't a sin for him to steal wallets.

Why, then, did Falstaff swear he must repent and give up his current life-style? Falstaff's bad debts to innkeepers and prostitutes are a continual reminder that he's failed to make money from his vocation. He thinks repentance might make him rich; but then again, so might a stolen wallet, fat with gold!

NOTE: Compare this to King Henry's situation for a moment. In taking the crown from King Richard II, Henry committed a criminal act, a sin. Now he feels sorry about it and wants to repent. He thinks the crusade will wash away his sin. But if you apply Falstaff's logic to Henry's situation, then the deposition wasn't illegal or sinful. Henry simply followed his vocation as a good politician by governing England. Why, then, does he feel such a compelling need to repent? Perhaps Henry isn't truly living up to his vocation. The continual uprisings and lawbreaking in the country are a constant reminder to Henry that he's not doing his job adequately. The nobles' rebellion, about to start in Scene 3, is kindled by Henry's failure to pay back his debts to his former supporters.

Now think about Prince Hal. He and Falstaff joke easily, but Hal never forgets to remind Falstaff how many times he's paid for Falstaff's entertainments.

Hal is generous to his friends, you discover, but he also makes sure they don't abuse his generosity.

Falstaff is a mirror for both Henry and Hal. Shakespeare is holding up that mirror, asking you to look into it. But he doesn't tell you how to judge what you're seeing—he only wants you to notice how complex life is. There are no simple explanations for people's behavior in a good play—or in life.

Lines 108–162

A thief named Poins enters, and tells Hal and "Monsieur Remorse" (Poins has obviously heard Falstaff's repentance act before) of a plot to rob merchants passing by Gad's Hill (a crossroads thirty miles from London) in the morning. He promises to fill their pockets full of crowns.

NOTE: A "crown" is an Elizabethan gold coin; it's also the symbol of kingship. Shakespeare puns on this double meaning throughout the play.

Falstaff joins Poins' plot eagerly, but Hal refuses— "Who, I rob? I a thief? Not I, by my faith." Falstaff dares him to, on pain of dishonor. Hal refuses. Falstaff threatens to become a traitor when Hal is king. "I care not," replies Hal. Falstaff tries to awaken Hal's honor and loyalty, but Hal doesn't seem tempted by such lofty ideals. This sets him in contrast to Hotspur, who, you've been told, is "the theme of honor's tongue."

This is the first time that the issue of how Hal will treat Falstaff later is brought up. Notice that although Hal gives Falstaff specific answers, Falstaff never takes Hal's warnings seriously.

Poins promises Falstaff to convince Hal to join the plot, and Falstaff goes cheerfully off to get drunk.

Lines 163–199

Poins has a trick planned, designed to make a fool of Falstaff, but he needs Hal's help to make it work. They'll disguise themselves and rob the robbers. Hal considers the plan coolly. What if they recognize us? he asks. Poins says he has special suits for disguises. What if they fight back? wonders Hal. Poins reassures him: Don't worry, they're all cowards. Bardolph, Peto, and Gadshill (the members of the thieving gang) will run away, and Falstaff will fight only as long as he thinks he has to. Hal finally agrees to this plan, and arranges to meet Poins the next day. Poins leaves.

NOTE: What are you to think of a Prince of Wales who steals money, even for fun? Readers have suggested several possible motives: 1. Hal wants to make a fool of Falstaff; 2. Falstaff, a robber himself, couldn't report the robbery, so Hal would be safe from recrimination from the court, and from scandal; 3. stealing from a thief is more like a form of rough justice, than like a real crime; or 4. Hal is acting out a family pattern of stealing crowns. Notice that Hal needed only a little reassurance that he wouldn't get caught (like Henry's getting popular support for his usurpation) in order to turn thief.

Lines 200–222

Alone, Hal switches from prose to courtly verse. He tells you a secret: His "loose behavior" is only a disguise. He has deliberately earned a bad reputation for himself, but he has his reformation planned. He shrewdly realizes that if he counterfeits villainy now, he'll look even better when his true self shines through.

NOTE: Hal's sudden revelation has bothered many readers. They think he's being coldhearted and calculating, disloyal to his friends. (These readers often think the same about King Henry!) Other readers see Hal more heroically, as a true student of kingship, who understands that he must put some distance between himself and his surroundings in order to observe them, to learn about the people and country he'll one day have to govern. Think about how modern politicians emphasize any experiences that prove they are truly "of the people." Even though Hal doesn't have to be elected to his job, he still seems to understand instinctively how to gain popular support.

ACT I, SCENE III

In Act I, Scene i, you saw King Henry consulting with his loyal advisers. Now you see him quarreling with his most troublesome subjects, the Percies. They have met to discuss Hotspur's refusal to surrender his Scottish prisoners.

NOTE: The Percies (Northumberland, Worcester, and Hotspur) were Henry's first and greatest supporters in his campaign against King Richard II. Because Henry was penniless when he returned from exile, he offered to repay the Percies for their help with power when he became king. So far Henry hasn't paid back his debts to the Percies, and they've decided that Henry never intended to. They see him as a scheming politician, using his friends and then casting them away when they're no longer useful.

The quarrel in this scene takes the form of three deliberate challenges to Henry's authority. Obviously, the Percies are up to something. The only Percy not involved in the conspiracy at this point is Hotspur—he's the innocent bait for Henry.

Lines 1–21

Henry is threatening to use his royal power against the Percies if they continue to disobey him. Worcester reminds Henry that the Percies gave him the very power he's now trying to use against them. Henry doesn't want to be reminded of this, however, and banishes Worcester from the court.

Notice how Henry's opening lines (lines 1–9) echo Hal's closing words in the previous scene. Hal promised that he will "imitate the sun"; Henry is promising to act like a royal lion, "Mighty and to be feared." Hal will lawfully inherit the crown, and so he has a right to use royal imagery. Henry, on the other hand, was placed on the throne with the Percies' help, and Worcester is here questioning Henry's right to use royal authority.

Worcester's image of making Henry "portly" with power may remind you of Falstaff's "portly" body. Henry's crown gives him stature and makes him a figure of authority; Falstaff's belly makes him physically imposing but also a figure of fun.

Lines 21–78

The quarrel resumes over whether or not Hotspur intended to send his Scottish prisoners to Henry. Northumberland defends Hotspur's disobedience by insisting that exaggerated rumors were spread by his detractors. Hotspur blames the king's messenger for bringing him a false report.

Once again you're being asked to question the accuracy of news and reputations. The Percies are using unverifiable reports as a way to challenge Henry's authority. Hotspur's speech about the messenger (lines 30–71) offers a good example of their strategy.

Hotspur reconstructs the end of the Scottish battle. He says he was bleeding and exhausted, leaning on his sword to keep from collapsing, when the neatly dressed messenger rode up. The messenger was bathed in perfume to cover up the nauseating smell of the dead bodies, and chattered about the unpleasantness of war. This "popinjay" (parrot) lord made Hotspur so impatient and angry

> To see him shine so brisk, and smell so sweet,
> And talk so like a waiting gentlewoman
> Of guns and drums and wounds

that Hotspur could only answer the cowardly lord's questions "neglectingly" and "indirectly."

Henry's loyal follower, Sir Walter Blunt, is embarrassed by this description and suggests that Henry might be better off if he forgot the entire incident. After what you've seen of Henry's character, it's hard to believe he'd send such a prissy lord as his representative to a battlefield. Could the story have been made up?

Nothing Hotspur says sounds rehearsed: The images flow from his memory on a flood of indignation. But perhaps Worcester invented this story in order to discredit Henry's image.

Lines 79–128

All through this scene Henry has been cold and angry, or scared. Now you discover why he's reacting so badly to the Percies—they're forcing him to make a

bargain over the Scottish prisoners, which is a great
insult to his royal status. They've made Henry an offer
they know he can't possibly agree to: Hotspur will
yield his prisoners only if Henry agrees to pay Glendower to free Mortimer. Glendower, however, is one
of Henry's greatest enemies, and Henry has no reason to want to save Mortimer (who is King Richard's
designated heir). To make matters worse, Mortimer
has married Glendower's daughter, and Hotspur is
married to Mortimer's sister.

Henry believes that Mortimer is a traitor, and pur-
posely lost the battle in Wales to Glendower. He flatly
refuses the Percies' proposal. "Shall we buy treason?"
the king asks in disbelief. Hotspur bursts out in a passionate defense of Mortimer's military prowess and
accuses Henry of slander.

Henry turns white with fury and calls Hotspur a
liar. He issues a curt order for Hotspur to deliver his
prisoners immediately, and rushes from the room. Is
this the behavior of a slick politician—getting in the
final word before slamming the door politely—or of a
man driven into a corner, having no place else to run?
The part probably could be played either way. Continue to study Henry's words and actions, to decide
how you'd play it.

Lines 129–151

Hotspur reacts to Henry's insult like a spoiled child
being punished: "An if the Devil come and roar for
them,/I will not send them." Northumberland re-
strains his hot-headed son from rushing after the king
to deliver this message in person.

Typically, Hotspur overreacts to insult by going to
extremes. He swears he'll start a campaign to overthrow Henry—"this unthankful King"—and place
Mortimer on the throne. He's willing to overthrow the

government to save a personal code of honor. Think about people you know who behave like Hotspur in an argument. Would you trust them in leadership roles?

Now that Henry is gone, Worcester baits Hotspur into joining a conspiracy to rebel against the king. He and Northumberland have already planned this coup. The first part of their scheme was to alienate Hotspur and Henry. So far their plan has worked perfectly.

Lines 152–196

Worcester (who returned after the king left) tells Hotspur that Mortimer is Richard's designated heir. Hotspur idealizes Richard, calling him a "sweet lovely rose" whereas Henry is a "thorn" in their sides. Hotspur's romanticism of Richard's reign is similar to Falstaff's idealization of youth. Hotspur doesn't notice the irony of idealizing Richard; the Percies rebelled against Richard to place Henry on the throne.

Worcester plays upon Hotspur's most vulnerable feature, his sense of honor. Worcester reminds Hotspur that their family has been blamed for Richard's death—not Henry. As a result, their family honor has been badly tarnished.

Hotspur fumes at this rankling thought. He calls his relatives hangmen, and scoffs at them for being "fooled, discarded, and shook off" by Henry since the deposition. (Remember that Hal has offered to make Falstaff his royal hangman. Will he turn his back on Falstaff as Henry seems to have turned his back on the Percies?) Hotspur urges his family to restore their "banished honors" before Henry has time to get them out of his way.

Lines 197–218

Worcester tells Hotspur that he has some deep and dangerous matters to discuss. Hotspur can't resist—danger and honor are his vocation.

Hotspur's imagination becomes inflamed thinking of the honor to be won by rebelling against Henry. He sees himself grappling with honor and danger, diving to the bottom of the sea or leaping to the moon to rescue "bright honor." These images are your first real indications that Hotspur's honor is his goddess, to whom he's totally committed. The language is energetic, with extremely physical images. Hotspur seems to draw his power from the very idea of honor.

Lines 219–270

Worcester and Northumberland have a hard time quieting Hotspur long enough to reveal their conspiracy plan. His father calls him a "wasp-stung and impatient fool," and many readers find this restless intensity one of Hotspur's most attractive features. It's certainly the one that causes him the most trouble. Northumberland fears that Hotspur will destroy their careful planning.

Hotspur calls Henry a "vile politician" and a "king of smiles." It shows how much he dislikes court politics, where calculation and cunning govern men's lives. Even today you hear political candidates claim that they hate playing the games that professional politicians play. Do you think it's possible for idealists to succeed in politics?

Lines 271–320

Hotspur finally agrees to listen to his uncle's plan. The Percies are going to join forces with Glendower, Mortimer, the Archbishop of York, and Douglas (the

Scottish general whom Hotspur just defeated). They'll
wait for the right opportunity and then strike against
the king.

Hotspur is sure it will be a noble plot because of the
caliber of the conspirators. He's willing to abide by the
decisions of others, unlike Hal, who cautiously questioned each detail of the plot Poins proposed to him.
Hotspur may be rebelling for honor, but notice that
the elder Percies aren't concerned about redeeming
their honor—they're more afraid that Henry will kill
them, partly so he won't have to be reminded of how
he came to wear the crown, and partly so he won't
have to share his power with them. The Percies' rebellion, then, is motivated by fear and a desire for honor;
it has nothing to do with politics or the good of
England.

The Percies are a very tightly knit family. They're
tightening a knot around Henry's crown, like a noose.
Hotspur can barely wait for the royal "sport" to
begin.

NOTE: Notice how the balance of justice has just
swung into reverse, against Henry. Readers tend to
find three different explanations for the Percy upris-
ing:

1.   Shakespeare's audience would have said that it
was part of Henry's due punishment for deposing
and murdering a rightful king. He's being punished
with a copy of his own crime, and nothing he can do
will stop it. Peace and order will return to England
only when a rightful king wears the crown once
more.

2. Some readers take a broad philosophical view and say that the rebellion is an inevitable consequence of the deposition, because history always repeats itself.

3. Others say that the rebellion resulted from the one major flaw in Henry's political campaign to become king: He depended on powerful lords and made them promises he never intended to keep. If you look at the Percies' motives, their conspiracy becomes a selfish bid for power by a group of dissatisfied lords who just want to share the power they helped to create. It has nothing to do with justice.

ACT II

ACT II, SCENE I

In this scene two carriers talk about the condition of England, and two thieves prepare the robbery at Gad's Hill.

Lines 1–47

Act I closed with Hotspur's rousing cry for action. As Act II opens a scruffy fellow is yawning and peering through the darkness with a lantern. It's sometime between two and four o'clock in the morning, in the stableyard of a hotel near Gad's Hill. Two carriers (deliverymen) are preparing to take men and goods to London. One carrier calls for the stable boy to help them. The stable boy calls back, "Anon, anon!" but he never appears. The two carriers complain about how badly the hotel has run down since its previous owner died.

> 2. *Car.:* This house is turned upside down since
>   Robin Ostler died.
> 1. *Car.:* Poor fellow never joyed since the price
>   of oats rose. It was the death of him.

NOTE: This scene seems to have little to do with Shakespeare's plot, but if you listen closely to the carriers' conversation you'll realize that the domestic disorder of the "house" (hotel) mirrors the political and social disorder of Henry's England, and the two "houses" that are trying to govern England—the king's family and the Percies. It also shows that the troubles at the head of the kingdom have trickled down to affect every level of society.

The hotel rooms stink and are infested with fleas that sting the guests. England, too, is infested—with thieves and traitors. The rebels feel stung by Henry's policies (see Act I, Scene iii, lines 245–246).

Robin Ostler died of poverty after prices rose. King Richard died partly because he overtaxed his subjects.

Notice the images of commerce and speed in this scene. At the hotel there are horses to harness, guests to awaken, journeys to take, business deals to make, and accounts to settle. Think about Henry's urgency to go on a crusade, to settle his account with God. The Percies have horses to spur, men to awaken to their cause, and debts to square with King Henry and Prince Hal.

Gadshill, a member of Poins' gang, enters the scene and tries to trick the carriers into giving him the lantern. The trick fails, but Gadshill succeeds in finding out that they're going to London that day, by way of Gad's Hill. Gadshill calls for the chamberlain (room attendant), who appears as the carriers depart.

Lines 48–97

You discover that the chamberlain is an informer who relays information to Gadshill about the hotel guests—who they are, where they're going, and how much money they are carrying.

Notice how the chamberlain's speedy entrance contrasts with the stable boy's reluctance to help the carriers with their horses. It almost seems that only thieves can command attention and respect in Henry's England. The honest, hardworking carriers are ignored by the hotel servants; the hotel guests are tricked and set up to be robbed by the thieves. This is another example of the disorder afflicting England.

Much of the dialogue in this scene is difficult to follow because it's written in Elizabethan criminal slang. Basically, Gadshill is making a comparison between two kinds of thieves: those who rob for "sport" (like Prince Hal, and perhaps Hotspur), and those who rob for a living and prey on the commonwealth (like Falstaff and the rebels). Then Gadshill changes his mind and decides that all thieves are alike. Keep that in mind as you watch Hal taking part in the Gad's Hill robbery.

Gadshill promises as a "true man" to pay the chamberlain for his information out of the robbery spoils. But the chamberlain would rather seal the bargain as a "false thief," because the word of honor of a thief is traditionally supposed to be stronger than the promises of honest men.

NOTE: Here the opposition between "true man" and "false thief" echoes King Henry's broken promises to the Percies. A thief is by definition a dishonest man; his intentions may be questioned, as well as his loyalty. Gadshill is lying when he says he's a "true man" because he's a thief. The chamberlain wishes him to swear truthfully, as he is a "false thief." King Henry is a thief who claims to be a true king, and he was disloyal to both King Richard and the Percies.

ACT II, SCENE II

The robberies committed in this scene are the tavern world's moral counterpart to the rebellions at court. Both Falstaff and Hotspur try to steal "crowns" and fail. Hal successfully steals "crowns," just as his father succeeded in stealing Richard's "crown."

It's four o'clock in the morning and robbery is being committed at Gad's Hill. Remember that Hal agreed to participate only because he and Poins intend to play a practical joke on Falstaff, by robbing him of the stolen money. The double robbery gives you a chance to examine the definitions of honor and cowardice in the play: Is it nobler to fight a battle until the bitter end, or to run away when you realize you're overpowered and bound to lose? This will become an important issue during the battle of Shrewsbury in Act V.

Lines 1–46

You've already heard Poins predict, in Act I, Scene ii, that Falstaff will behave like a coward during the robbery. If Falstaff fights "longer than he sees reason, I'll forswear arms," Poins declared then, implying that a man is honorable only if he fights until the battle's end, regardless of who is winning. But there's another point of view, which says that honor is one thing, but saving your life is another, and it's better to live in dishonor than die for the sake of a good reputation.

NOTE: For centuries readers have been arguing over whether or not Falstaff behaves like a coward in this scene. Some readers see the fat knight quivering with fear and roaring for mercy as he runs away from the buckram-suited robbers, and call him an absolute coward. Other readers are more sympathetic to Falstaff, and see him struggling to maintain his dignity in the face of what he sees as grave danger—he's willing to lose the stolen money but not his life. Look at the evidence for both sides of this argument, and decide for yourself.

As the scene begins, Poins and Hal seem determined to get as many laughs as possible at Falstaff's expense. They hide his horse, and then hide themselves to watch the "fat-kidneyed rascal" struggle uphill on foot. When Falstaff enters, he's cursing Poins and Hal for removing his horse:

> Eight yards of uneven ground is threescore and ten miles afoot with me, and the stony-hearted villains know it well enough. A plague upon it when thieves cannot be true one to another!

Some readers see Falstaff's speech as positive proof that he's terrified of being alone in the middle of the night, and he insults his friends only to give himself confidence. The longer he's left alone, the more frantic his calls for help and oaths against Poins become. When Hal finally appears, Falstaff covers up his fear with jokes.

Falstaff's defenders point out that the old knight would be too terrified to speak if he were really afraid. Having guessed that Poins hid his horse, Falstaff is merely angry and disheartened to discover that his best friends aren't loyal to him or mindful of his old age and obesity. Any fear Falstaff might show is natural, a simple instinct for self-preservation. After all, who wouldn't be nervous, stranded on a dangerous, unlit road famous for highway robbery? When Hal appears, Falstaff firmly demands an explanation for the prank, insults the prince, and jokes about his weight. A true coward wouldn't have the self-possession to recover that quickly.

Notice that Falstaff is deserted by his friends just before the robbery. King Henry has just been deserted by his former allies, the Percies. Perhaps Hotspur would do well to place less faith in his co-conspirators, in such a world of shaky loyalties.

Lines 48–78

Gadshill arrives and warns the thieves that the travelers are approaching. They put on disguises, take their battle positions, and wait. Peto wonders how many travelers they'll be up against.

> Gadshill: Some eight or ten.
> Falstaff: Zounds, will they not rob us?
> Prince: What, a coward, Sir John Paunch?
> Falstaff: Indeed, I am not John of Gaunt,
> your grandfather, but yet no coward . . .

Falstaff's detractors refer to literary tradition to support their view of Falstaff as a coward. One literary device used in comedy, they say, is that any character who claims he's not a coward is soon proved to be one. There's no reason to think that Falstaff is any different.

Falstaff's defenders remember that he's an old military captain who would be practical and weigh the odds of winning a battle when his troops are outnumbered. This shows Falstaff to be a cautious leader, concerned for his troops' safety. Keep this feature in mind when you see the real battle in Act V.

Lines 79–91

Poins and Hal hide and put on their disguises. The travelers arrive meanwhile, and the rest of the thieves rob them. What does Falstaff do?

Some readers imagine Falstaff standing cowardly on the sidelines, shouting encouragement to the real thieves and insults to their victims. They say he doesn't actually take part in the robbery.

Other readers point to Shakespeare's stage direction in the text, which simply says, "Here they rob them and bind them." There's no indication that Falstaff lets his friends do all the work. They say he participates in the robbery along with Bardolph, Peto, and Gadshill.

Lines 92–110

The thieves divide their loot. Falstaff accuses Hal and Poins, who he thinks have slipped away, of being cowards. Then Hal and Poins (disguised) emerge from hiding and attack the thieves. All but Falstaff run away at once; Falstaff strikes a few blows and then runs away, leaving the money on the ground.

Poins' prediction has come true. But is this proof that Falstaff is a coward? Hal announces, just in case anyone missed the point, that the thieves "are all scattered and possessed with fear." Poins shakes his head and laughs at Falstaff, "How the fat rogue roared!" You have to admit that Falstaff certainly seems to be behaving like a coward now, but you could also say that he's behaving as any self-respecting criminal would if he were caught in the act—running away to avoid arrest and hanging. He isn't a coward if he's a practical man determined to escape the gallows.

Still, the thieves did run away, like a losing army afraid to hang around for an honorable surrender. Do only thieves act this way? Watch as the Percies' rebellion progresses: Some of them, too, will defect the minute their side seems to be losing. Where will that leave the "honorable thief" Hotspur? Will he, like Falstaff, run to save his life?

Even though he runs away, Falstaff manages to do his country some service at Gad's Hill. Hal says he "lards the lean earth as he walks," sweating from exertion or fear. (The Elizabethans thought perspiration was melting body fat.) The fat knight, therefore, feeds England. Later you'll see Hotspur feeding the worms at Shrewsbury with his lifeless body.

NOTE: What are you to think of a prince who robs people, even if it's just in fun? Some readers say that Hal's joke is morally indefensible because it sets a bad example for his future subjects; others excuse Hal's behavior on the grounds that the people he robs are themselves thieves.

The Prince of Wales does play a mean practical joke on a fat old man. Falstaff may complain of losing his breath, but he never stops talking. At the scene's beginning he swears he can't move another inch without dying of exhaustion, but by the end of the scene he's running away like a young man. Hal's joke doesn't seem to have harmed anything more serious than Falstaff's dignity.

Notice that Hal takes command of the thieves, even though he's never committed highway robbery before. Not only do the thieves unquestioningly accept his authority, but his plan works perfectly, and the prince gets what he came to Gad's Hill for: "argument for a week, laughter for a month, and a good jest forever." This shows him to be a good leader, and a man who knows how to get what he wants. Knowing this, you may take him more seriously than his father does.

ACT II, SCENE III

The last time you saw Hotspur he was passionately riding off to start the rebellion against King Henry. Now you see another side of him, at home, reading a letter and talking with his wife.

Lines 1–35

The Percies have obviously been gathering support for their rebellion. Everything is going according to plan: Glendower, Mortimer, the Archbishop of York, and Douglas have agreed to meet them on the ninth of next month, ready to march against the king.

But Hotspur is reading aloud a letter from one lord who doesn't think the Percies have a very good chance of winning, and refuses to join the conspiracy. He offers reasonable excuses: The allies can't be trusted, the timing for the march isn't the best, and he fears they underestimate the power and size of the king's army.

Hotspur is furious; he doesn't think these are very good reasons at all. Hotspur has no patience for men who think twice about consequences. Think about Hal's careful questioning of Poins in Act I, Scene ii. Hal wouldn't join in the robbery until he was satisfied that there was no chance of getting into trouble or having the plan fail. Do you believe it's cowardly to be cautious before you undertake a dangerous action? Some people are cautious to make sure they won't get hurt; others are cautious to make sure they will succeed. Hal believes in safety and in winning; Hotspur, however, believes mostly in sticking with a cause.

Hotspur calls this lord a "frosty-spirited rogue," in other words, a wet blanket. He doesn't stop to think if any of the lord's objections might contain truth. (You'll see, in fact, in Act IV, that every one of the objections comes true.) But Hotspur's code of honor won't allow him to doubt his cause or distrust his allies.

No one, not even a hero, likes to think he's about to do something foolish. As the lord's warning begins to sink in, Hotspur rants and mocks him with increasing impatience and fury:

> . . . By the Lord, our plot is a good plot as ever was laid; our friends true and constant: a good plot, good friends, and full of expectation; an excellent plot, very good friends . . .

Notice the repetitions in Hotspur's speech. Is Hotspur genuinely amazed that anyone would disagree with him? Does his self-confidence sound forced to you? The code of honor says he must be brave and loyal at any cost. What if Hotspur is scared and can't admit it? Haven't you seen people trapped by the need to appear "macho"? All that Hotspur seems worried about is that Henry might be told of the conspiracy, and the rebels will thus lose the element of surprise. Hotspur can't look back; he realizes that war is now inevitable. He does take one precaution—he speeds his departure. As his wife enters, Hotspur is calling for his horse.

Lines 36–124

Lady Percy shows you the other side of Hotspur's courage. Hotspur won't tell her what's wrong, but she knows something is happening, something dangerous, because Hotspur can't eat, and on the few occasions he can fall asleep he has nightmares. She says he spends all day by himself, brooding. Is he carefully planning his battle strategies, a young man thoroughly engaged in a great project? Or are these the symptoms of anxiety and fear?

Hotspur doesn't want to listen to his wife's catalogue of the symptoms he can't admit to having. On stage, the actor playing Hotspur might stare ahead, thinking about the rebellion, not listening to her loving expression of concern. As soon as she's finished, he starts calling for his horse again. She calls him a parrot, and says he's "mad-headed" and full of "spleen" (sullen and moody). She's charming and gentle with him, but the prince of honor refuses to tell his own wife about the rebellion. Honor requires that he doesn't betray his friends or seem like a coward, even to his wife.

But the young man underneath the shining armor seems very worried indeed. He knows what kinds of risks he's taking. In his sleep he's been remembering every military strategy he's ever devised, listing weapons, counting the dead—"all the currents of a heady fight" float through his unconscious mind.

Neither the lord's cautious warning nor his wife's loving appeals can keep Hotspur from carrying on the crusade against Henry. "We must have bloody noses and cracked crowns [heads]" he cries. Honor spurs him on. He cannot or will not listen to second opinions; his safety isn't important. But from now on Hotspur will systematically be stripped of his illusions about honor, until he lies dead on the battlefield. You'll have to decide whether it was worth it.

ACT II, SCENE IV

This scene in the Eastcheap tavern consists of four major parts: 1. Hal and Francis; 2. Falstaff's "incomprehensible lies"; 3. the tavern play; and 4. the Sheriff.

Lines 1–113

While waiting for Falstaff and the thieves to return to Eastcheap, Hal tells Poins that he spent fifteen minutes in the cellar of the tavern talking to the drawers (waiters). He's learned their slang and is now "sworn brother" to them all. The drawers have crowned Hal the "king of courtesy" (the most gallant knight), and swear their allegiance to him when he becomes king of England.

Hal finds this funny, but he also finds it honorable: "I tell thee, Ned," laughs the prince, "thou hast lost much honor that thou wert not with me in this action." Is Hal joking about honor at the expense of the drawers (as he laughed at Falstaff at Gad's Hill)? Or does his laughter disguise a serious purpose? What kind of honor can Hal expect to win in a tavern cellar? It's not the kind of honor Hotspur intends to win in battle, although it may make Hal famous throughout Eastcheap. Hotspur's honor is bound up in military fame and glory. Hal's honor in the tavern seems to be part of his education in kingship: He's learning about the men he'll one day have to rule.

To prove how well he knows the drawers, Hal decides to play a trick on one of them, Francis. If we stand in different rooms and call Francis at the same time, Hal predicts to Poins, he'll end up caught in the middle, unable to decide which caller to serve. The trick works exactly as Hal predicts. Poins and the prince have a good laugh over the unfortunate drawer's behavior.

NOTE: Notice the imagery of time in this episode. All Hal's questions to Francis relate to time—how long his apprenticeship will last, how old he is, when he gets paid. His last question is, "What time is it?" And Francis answers, "Anon, anon," soon. Perhaps Hal is wondering how much longer he can stay in the tavern world before he has to return to the court.

If you look at Hal's practical joke from a personal point of view, as many readers do, you can say that Hal is behaving like a bully, heartlessly toying with another person. You can say that Hal is being devious, too, because he can't openly ask people about themselves.

But you can also look at the practical joke as a mirror image of Hal's situation. Like Francis, Hal is pulled in two directions at once. Francis is unable to distinguish which caller is more important, so he gets stuck in the middle. Hal is being pulled in opposite directions by Falstaff in the tavern world and by his father in the court world. If Hal is consciously creating this mirror image, he's taking a good look at his own situation and laughing at its absurdity. All Francis could do was to tell his tormentors "soon." All you've heard Hal say so far is that he'll decide which world he belongs in, soon.

Hal laughs at Francis for knowing "fewer words than a parrot." Calling Francis a parrot reminds Hal of Hotspur. (Remember that Hotspur called the king's messenger a parrot, and Lady Percy has just called Hotspur a parrot.) Hal muses that life in Hotspur's house must be very boring, as boring as Francis' life of waiting on tables. Hal imagines Hotspur and his wife having only one topic of conversation at the breakfast table: war. "I am not yet of Percy's mind, the Hotspur of the North," says Hal—implying that he will be, someday. He cynically imagines Hotspur killing six or seven dozen men before breakfast and then, an hour later, calling it a "trifle." Hal has never met Hotspur, but we can see from this how their attitudes toward war differ: Hotspur lives only for military honor, while Hal thinks that's too narrow a life-style. Thinking about the single-minded Hotspur makes Hal yearn for the robust, contradictory Falstaff.

Lines 114–376

Hal and Poins have just baited the wordless Francis; now they'll bait the wordy Falstaff as the second part of their robbery trick begins.

You just heard Hotspur in Act II, Scene iii, calling for bloody noses and cracked crowns. Falstaff delivers some of them now.

Falstaff's entrance on stage (with Bardolph, Peto, and Gadshill) is a moment of pure drama. Picture the fat knight and his crew in torn and bloody clothes, groaning from the wounds they sustained at Gad's Hill; notice how their swords are hacked and how they gasp for breath.

Falstaff is so short of breath as he enters that at first he sounds almost like Francis, with only two phrases in his head: "A plague of all cowards." and "Give me a cup of sack [sherry]." His voice is weak as he curses the evilness of the world and mutters about vengeance and virtue.

Hal asks him what's wrong, with an innocent air.

"A king's son!" bellows Falstaff. "If I do not beat thee out of thy kingdom with a dagger of lath. . . . You Prince of Wales." Falstaff threatens to banish Hal from England with a prop sword. At the end of this scene, however, you'll see Hal promise to banish Falstaff.

Falstaff accuses Poins and Hal of cowardice and disloyalty, charging them with the very insults they used against him in Act II, Scene ii. Falstaff asks Hal and Poins if they dare to call running away the "backing of your friends." Notice that he's beginning to sound like Hotspur did when he was reading the cowardly lord's letter.

Hal pretends he doesn't know what Falstaff is talking about. And Falstaff's "incomprehensible lies" begin. They're epic in scope, the stuff of legends. Poins has predicted Falstaff's behavior perfectly, as you will see.

Falstaff launches heroically into his account of the battle of Gad's Hill. Although shamefully deserted by Hal and Poins, Falstaff says, he and his men stole the sum of 1000 pounds; then they were robbed of the money by 100 men. Falstaff claims he escaped only by a miracle. He shows Hal and Poins his bloody clothes and hacked sword as proof. Hal and Poins are amazed at the extravagance of his performance. (You can think of this as a parody of Hotspur and his description of the king's messenger in Act I, Scene iii.) On stage Falstaff usually acts out his brave fight against an ever-changing number of thieves. Toward the end, 52 men set upon Falstaff at once. If I'm lying, declares Falstaff, "I am a bunch of radish!"

Hal casually asks Falstaff if he killed any of the thieves. Falstaff sighs and admits he "peppered two of them . . . two rogues in buckram suits . . . if I tell thee a lie, spit in my face, call me horse" The numbers of men in buckram multiply rapidly now: 2, 4, 7, 9, 11 . . . "O monstrous!" cries Hal, "Eleven buckram men grown out of two!"

Right when Falstaff looks and sounds his most heroic, Hal stops his lies cold, with the truth: "These lies are like their father that begets them—gross as a mountain, open, palpable." "Art thou mad?" demands Falstaff, "Is not the truth the truth?"

NOTE: One of the main themes of the play is how people deceive themselves and others with lies and false reports that they swear are true. Elsewhere in the play the report is almost always believed by the hearer, but here, nobody is fooled by Falstaff's lies.

Hal and Falstaff call each other names. (Look at their imagery: Falstaff calls Hal various shrunken objects, such as a "starveling"; Hal calls Falstaff all sorts of gigantic objects, including a "huge hill of flesh." Hal finds Falstaff's lies disgusting, and Falstaff thinks he's beaten Hal. The two men are at a critical moment in their friendship, jockeying for power over one another. The rest of this scene defines their status toward each other.

Hal at last tells Falstaff the truth about the trick. He's furious at Falstaff for pretending to be wounded in a great battle. (Keep this in mind later, when Falstaff fakes death at Shrewsbury.) Hal challenges Falstaff to get out of the verbal trap he's built for himself.

By this time Falstaff, can appear either cowed or pleased with his cleverness. He pauses and then announces, "By the Lord, I knew ye as well as he that made ye." His audience is stunned. Falstaff continues, all innocence, to explain why he ran away like a coward: I knew it was you, Hal. Like a lion (a kingly image) I can tell the true prince, by instinct, from the false thief.

A messenger arrives at the tavern with news: Hal is told of the Percy rebellion and ordered to report to his father the next morning; his time in the tavern world is up. Falstaff asks Hal if he's horribly afraid or thrilled at the prospect of fighting his father's enemies. Some readers see this as Falstaff playing the old soldier, coaching a young and inexperienced one. Others believe Falstaff is proving to be a coward once more, by imagining what he'd do in Hal's place.

Lines 377–487:

Falstaff and Hal agree to rehearse Hal's upcoming interview with Henry. Falstaff plays the king, choosing a three-legged stool for his throne, a cushion for his crown, and the hacked-up sword for his scepter. Hal sees the comic absurdity of these props:

> Thy state is taken for a joined-stool, thy golden sceptre for a leaden dagger, and thy precious rich crown for a pitiful bald crown.

Here is the crown imagery in its most ironic form. Hal, the future king of England, clearly recognizes the difference between the majesty of true kingship and its travesty at the hands of Falstaff. The crown of England becomes a bald head, a threadbare cushion, and worst of all, a fake. You can also see this as a commentary on the state of kingship whenever the king is a thief.

Falstaff relishes this chance to do some real acting. He cleverly invents props, finds makeup in the bleary-eyed effect of drinking sack, and chooses a suitably tragic tone of voice, something he could have gotten out of the sixteenth-century theater repertory—a parody of a king in a ranting tragedy.

NOTE: Notice how sharply this brings forward your image of Henry as a usurper and a clever politician. Falstaff shows you a king who's floundering in circumstances beyond his control, making do with whatever is at hand, inventing strategies on the spot. Falstaff shows you a politician who knows how to adjust his tone of voice to suit his audience, and carefully watches for the effects he has on them.

Falstaff sits on the joint-stool throne, and addresses Hal. His entire speech is a parody of what Henry will say in Act III Scene ii. He takes a highly moral attitude toward the wayward young prince and is shocked at the company Hal keeps. He warns Hal that he's wasting his precious youth, and wonders why Hal, who seems to be his son, has such a bad reputation. This question raises a moral question about Hal's youthful rebellion: When the King of England is a thief, will his son be one, too? Falstaff is able to guess exactly what Henry will say; it shouldn't be hard, since it's the same argument fathers have always had with their sons. They're afraid their sons won't live up to their high expectations, and scared that their own faults will show up in their sons.

Now Falstaff starts to play with Hal. "Henry" tells Hal that he's noticed just one virtuous man in his company, a "goodly portly man, i' faith, and a corpulent." Keep him, urges "Henry," and banish all the rest of your friends. Falstaff probably suspects that Hal may leave him behind after the real interview the next day. He's indirectly begging Hal not to leave him behind later when the reformation comes.

Hal now demands that they exchange roles. "Depose me?" asks "Henry" in mock horror. If you make a better king than I do, he retorts, hang me upside down. This is a central action of the play: the deposition of one king in order to place a "better" king on the throne. The penalty for proving to be a false king—a traitor—is hanging. It's ironic that Falstaff should call Hal's taking up the crown a deposition: Hal is the only candidate for kingship in the play who won't have to steal the crown to wear it.

As "king," Hal calls Falstaff every offensive name he can think of, referring to his obesity, thieving, vanity, drunkenness, and cunning. Hal demands to know what worth Falstaff has. This is the same sort of vicious, negative attitude that the Percies take toward King Henry—seeing him as only the cunning, pompous politician.

Falstaff pretends not to know to whom Hal is referring. "That villainous abominable misleader of youth, Falstaff, that old white-beared Satan," Hal replies coldly. Falstaff defends himself, pleading the vices of old age and claiming the license of knighthood. No, insists Falstaff, banish everyone else, but "banish plump Jack, and banish all the world!" Hal replies simply, "I do, I will."

NOTE: These lines have astonished readers for years. Some say it proves absolutely that Hal is no better than his hard-hearted, calculating politician of a father, that Hal has been using Falstaff badly. Other readers prefer to see Hal as the future king who must cast aside the immorality Falstaff represents, no matter how attractive he is as a companion. They say that if Falstaff is shocked, then it's his own fault for believing that Hal could ever be like him and still be a true prince.

At the end of *Henry IV, Part 2*, the newly crowned King Henry V will do exactly what he's promised here, and banish Falstaff from his presence.

Lines 488–558

As Hal speaks his fateful words, a knocking is heard offstage. It's a symbol that reality is about to take over. The pressures and responsibilities of the court are calling, and Hal's apprenticeship with Falstaff is over.

Bardolph answers the door and returns with the news that a sheriff and one of the carriers wish to search the house, to look for the stolen Gad's Hill money. Falstaff begs Hal not to betray him, not yet anyway. "Never call a true piece of gold a counterfeit," Falstaff counsels, as he hides behind a curtain.

Hal, however, surprisingly lies and tells the sheriff that Falstaff isn't there. He's no idealist; he's willing to lie if it serves a practical purpose. In spite of his recent harsh words, he must still feel affection for Falstaff, and so he saves him.

The fate Falstaff has always tried to avoid just came knocking at the door; in the face of grave danger, Falstaff hid. When Hal pulls back the curtain, Falstaff is snoring just as he was at the opening of Act I, Scene ii. Notice that he hides like a coward, but falls asleep like a man sure of his friends, with complete confidence in Hal. Just for good measure, Hal picks Falstaff's pocket. The practical joker in him still lives.

The tavern world has just come full circle, beginning and ending with Falstaff's snores. The next lines Prince Hal speaks look forward to the court. He promises that he will give Falstaff a military command, a company of foot soldiers (to get even with him for the "incomprehensible lies," perhaps). He promises to repay the stolen money with interest, and, with all his accounts settled, he leaves for his father's court.

ACT III

ACT III, SCENE I

The action shifts from Eastcheap to Glendower's castle in Wales. This scene is structured like a miniature drama with its own rising and falling action. Its atmosphere is unlike any other scene in the play.

Glendower, Hotspur, and Mortimer meet to sign a contract that divides England into three parts. Hotspur will rule the north of England and Scotland; Mortimer will rule the southeast of England, and Glendower will rule southwestern England and Wales.

NOTE: Notice how this contrasts with Henry's wish to have his people "march all one way." Henry's political ideas are those of an Elizabethan monarch or a modern candidate for president—a desire for a strong nation ruled by a strong leader. But the rebels want England for themselves and are dividing it up to satisfy personal needs for power. There's no political discussion in this scene, just a quarrel among three thieves (and one politician, Worcester, who probably designed the plan). They're so confident of overthrowing the king that they're sharing the spoils before committing the crime.

How would you react to hearing that the heads of a leading political party want to overthrow the government and divide up your country? Shakespeare gives us a series of clues as to how he and his audience would have felt.

Lines 1–13

The rebels' confused entrance in this scene should be contrasted to the formality of the king's court, and to the comfortable drunken sprawl of the tavern. In fact, in most stage productions the tables and chairs from the previous tavern scene are left onstage for the rebels' meeting—clearly linking themes between the two scenes.

The rebels can't decide who should sit down first and where they should sit. In the presence of royalty, the king would normally sit first and arrange his lords formally according to their ranks. As King Richard II's designated heir, then, Mortimer should take the royal initiative, and sit first. As host, Glendower ought to be granted the privilege of seating his guests. But notice that Hotspur takes charge of the seating arrangements. From this moment on everything Hotspur says and does in this scene threatens to break up the conspiracy.

Although the rebels are still confident and hopeful for the future, there's something disconcerting in the fact that Hotspur has lost the map of England they've been consulting. It's one indication of the disorder the rebels represent in the play. It may also be a sign that they've lost sight of England—her best interests—in their struggle for power.

Lines 14–79

Glendower and Hotspur quarrel over the Welshman's magical abilities. Glendower defends himself as fiercely as you've seen Hotspur defend his honor in other scenes. Their relationship in this scene depends mostly on whether you think Glendower really is a magician or not. You can see him as a wise magician whose quiet self-control outshines Hotspur's childish taunts; or you can see Glendower as a crackpot whose egotistical boasts and inane prophecies irritate Hotspur's honest and direct nature. If Glendower is a magician, then Hotspur is reacting to him as a rival; if Glendower is a fake, then Hotspur is reacting to him as a fool, and their relationship becomes parallel to Hal and Falstaff's.

Glendower boasts that when he was born the earth "shaked like a coward"—there was an earthquake, and the ground ran away from his feet in fear. Hotspur retorts that the earth merely had indigestion, and belched. These references to trembling cowards and digestive processes sound much like the images used to describe Falstaff.

Notice that in the middle of the rebel war council Shakespeare puts the imagery of disease and disorder in their mouths. You're not to forget that these men are planning to murder a king and butcher a country.

Glendower next boasts that he can command the devil. Hotspur scolds him, like Hal scolding Falstaff after one of his monstrous lies. Glendower retaliates with some hard facts that even Hotspur can't deny: he's already beaten King Henry's army three times in battle. Henry was sent home "bootless" and "weather-beaten," like a frail man overcome by a storm. The "bootless" image recalls many of the thieves' jokes in Act II, Scenes i and ii, and the image of Henry as a man overcome by the stormy power of the Welshman recalls the news of Mortimer's defeat in Act I, Scene i.

Lines 80–157

Mortimer intervenes and turns their attention back to the map of England, which Glendower has finally recovered. Hotspur argues that Glendower's share of the country is larger than his own. Their argument quickly degenerates into a childish squabble:

Hotspur:	I'll have it so. A little charge will do it.
Glendower:	I will not have it alt'red.
Hotspur:	Will you not?
Glendower:	No, nor you shall not.
Hotspur:	Who shall say me nay?
Glendower:	Why, that I will.

Next, the two great generals insult each other's ear for music and poetry. Glendower says he loves to sing English songs, and Hotspur retorts that the songs sound harsh and grating to him.

Glendower finally concedes the boundary to Hotspur, but Hotspur isn't a gracious winner; he further insults Glendower by saying he'd willingly give three times that amount of land to a friend, but he'll haggle with anyone else over the smallest fraction.

Lines 158–204

Glendower leaves to fetch Mortimer's and Hotspur's wives, so they can say good-bye before they leave for Shrewsbury.

While Glendower is out of the room, Mortimer and Worcester take turns scolding Hotspur for his rudeness toward Glendower. His impatience, they tell him, sometimes makes him seem courageous, but more often it shows "Defect of manners, want of government,/Pride, haughtiness, opinion, and disdain." Hotspur listens, against his will, to them listing the perils of his single-mindedness, and he sulks. As you listen to this lecture, you can compare Hotspur's faults to Hal's good points. Prince Hal has all the qualities Hotspur lacks, as his encounter with the drawers has already demonstrated.

Lines 205–288

Glendower returns with the wives, and the tense atmosphere becomes relaxed and romantic. Mortimer's wife sings in the musical language of the Welsh, accompanied by music that Glendower magically produces. There's peace in the magician's house, before the storm of battle begins. But Hotspur, the man of action, breaks the spell and calls for his horse.

ACT III, SCENE II

You saw Falstaff and Prince Hal rehearsing Hal's royal interview. Now Hal is in the palace, kneeling in front of his father, listening to a lecture on his irresponsible behavior. This scene is placed directly in the middle of the play, and it sums up many themes: authority and rebellion; kingship and politics; the education of a prince; and the relationship between a father and his son.

NOTE: As you judge Henry's statements, place them against the background of political events in the play. He sees Hal from two points of view—that of a king and that of a father.

As a king, it's his duty to punish criminals and traitors because they upset peace and order in the commonwealth. But Henry sees himself as once a "traitor," so it's hard for him to punish others. The Percies—who were rebels against the old king—went free and unpunished when their candidate, Henry, took over.

Henry has tried to maintain law and order in the kingdom, but no matter how hard he tries, disorder and fighting break out. Then his own son becomes a thief. His old supporters turn against him and embark on a new rebellion. A new set of traitors is born. The kingdom is in danger of collapsing once again.

King Henry is failing to maintain law and order, to carry out his obligations to his subjects. But he's trying, and as a father, he needs his son's support. This interview is also King Henry's way of finding out whether or not he can rely on Prince Hal.

Lines 1–30

Henry demands an explanation for Hal's riotous living. Hal simply blames his youth for some of it, and the rest on rumors and false reports that make him sound worse than he really is. Hal may be learning about kingship in the tavern world, but he doesn't take this opportunity to make Henry see it that way.

Lines 31–96

Henry tells Hal how hard he worked to get where he is today. (Isn't this a typical father's line?) He had to steal "all courtesy from heaven" (notice how this contrasts with the drawers' crowning Hal as "king of courtesy"). Henry had to "dress" himself in humility to convince the people to give their allegiance to him. (Hal has just done something like this—dressed himself in buckram—but you don't hear him boasting of it to his father.) Henry says he kept out of the public eye most of the time so that when he did make an appearance in a crowd, his presence, like a comet illuminating the night sky, struck the people with awe and wonder. He understood that in order to be a king you have to act like one.

You've already heard Hal's plan for a similar campaign strategy, in his soliloquy at the end of Act I, Scene ii. Hal intends to make his reformation "glitter" over his former bad reputation, just as Henry describes. But again, Hal keeps silent about this lesson in kingship he has already learned.

Henry then compares Hal with King Richard, who "Mingled his royalty with capering fools" until the people were sick of looking at him, and scorned him. Henry tells Hal that he, too, has lost his royal status by mixing with the wrong people.

Look at the imagery of Henry's speech, with its references to stealing, play-acting, and the importance of making the right effect. These are all lessons that Hal has already learned in the tavern with Falstaff. Many readers see Henry's speech as another elaborate justification of why he stole the crown. Like a man with a guilty conscience, he must keep retelling this story. You know that this is one crime Hal can't commit, because he'll inherit the crown. Other readers see

Henry's speech as a bitter and angry outburst, lashing out both at his "almost alien" son Hal, and at current events, which threaten to take away everything he has worked so hard to win.

The king cries over Hal: "Not an eye/But is weary of thy common sight,/Save mine, which has desired to see thee more." When Hal speaks, he simply promises to behave himself in the future. He doesn't show any regret for being at odds with his father. Is Hal behaving with youthful smugness, or are his answers polite and circumspect, as befits a royal heir? In either case, Hal doesn't tell Henry anything more than the barest facts. Remember that his reformation was designed to astonish his father as well as the rest of England.

Lines 97–131

Right now, continues Henry, you're acting like Richard, and Hotspur's acting like me when I started to campaign against Richard. He deserves to be king more than you do. I once turned my friends into Richard's enemies, just as Hotspur is turning my enemies into his friends. Hotspur, like a young god of war, is leading them into battle against me. He scornfully tells his son, you might as well join them.

Lines 132–162

Maybe it's Henry's claim that Hotspur would make a better king, or maybe it's the idea that Henry thinks Hal would fight against his own father, but Henry's speech finally triggers an emotional reaction in his aloof young son. No, answers Hal, it won't be that way. When the time comes, Hal assures his father, I'll put on a disguise of blood and force Hotspur to "render every glory up" in battle.

Hal is promising his father that he'll be as good a king's son as ever lived, that he'll equal and then surpass Hotspur. Hal chooses the traditional challenge for knights—single combat.

NOTE: Even though Hal is living up to the code of chivalry, look at the images he uses: "redeem," "exchange," "factor," "engross," "call him to so strict account," "render up," "reckoning," and "cancels all bands." Understanding that honor and reputation are commodities, he intends to exchange Hotspur's honor for his own.

Lines 163–183

King Henry is relieved to find Hal loyal, and he gives him command of one-third of the royal army. The interview is over, and so is the tug-of-war between the tavern and the court. From now on, the fight will be between Hal and Hotspur, not Henry and Falstaff.

ACT III, SCENE III

This is a scene about "reckonings"—all of the debts accumulated so far in the tavern are coming due, as the battle of Shrewsbury approaches.

In Eastcheap, Falstaff is playing "Monsieur Remorse" to Bardolph and quarreling with the hostess.

Lines 1–53

Falstaff is depressed. He's usually played drunk here. He looks like he's just lost his best friend. He asks Bardolph if he looks like he's losing weight. Is Falstaff too depressed even to eat, or is he still complaining about having to walk at Gad's Hill? "Do I not dwindle?" he asks. No he hasn't, Bardolph says, not one ounce. Yet his strength is failing, Falstaff insists. He wants to repent—again—he wants to reckon up his losses with God.

Long ago, Falstaff remembers, I led a virtuous life (well, virtuous enough). But now I live "out of all order, out of all compass." He probably looks ruefully now at his belly and his wine bottle. He's still "fat Jack," and he still lives out of order—outside the social and moral order of the court. He no longer recognizes himself as a member of a society he's lived in for sixty-odd years. Prince Hal has banished him. His hope for the future is gone. Low as he feels, he makes himself feel better by insulting Bardolph. He's been paying for Bardolph's upkeep for thirty-two years.

Lines 54–86

The hostess is a generous woman and a hardworking wife who runs an honest business. You learn that Falstaff owes her 24 pounds and the balance of his charge account bill for food and drink at the tavern.

As she enters, Falstaff may sense that she's come to collect her money. To divert her from bringing up the subject, he accuses her of picking his pocket. He knows that there were only restaurant bills and a piece of candy there to be taken, but he swears to her that he was robbed of a family signet ring and a good deal of money.

The hostess fights back spiritedly. Her strategy is to confront him with reality, with how much money and kindness he owes her. Notice how similar the hostess' strategy with Falstaff is to Lady Percy's with Hotspur. Both women are realistic but try to tease a confession from the men. Their efforts fail, but they make it clear how well they understand the men. Hotspur and Falstaff both resist the women's charms.

Falstaff boasts that a ring worth a fortune was stolen from his pocket, implying that he could have paid her back if it hadn't been stolen. Hal, however, had told her the ring was practically worthless, and she believes Hal.

Is Falstaff behaving like a con man or like a good military strategist? Either way, he's childishly evading his responsibilities, and transferring his anger and depression over Hal onto the innocent hostess.

Lines 87–92

In performance, when Hal enters with Peto, both dressed for war, you suddenly see the sharp contrast with Falstaff's sprawling, slovenly form. You see Falstaff at his most disreputable and Hal in his most royal uniform.

NOTE: A few lines before Hal's entrance, Falstaff shouts to the hostess, ''How? the prince is a Jack [a knave, a two-faced rascal], a sneak-up. 'Sblood, an he were here, I would cudgel him like a dog if he would say so'' (that the ring was worthless). The Prince of Wales enters immediately afterward. There are two ways to play this. Falstaff can say these lines deliberately, knowing that Hal is approaching and will hear them. Or Hal's entrance can follow the speech as an ironic coincidence, embarrassing Falstaff just when he's making a bold and impudent statement. He'd have only a split second in which to turn his roaring into a playful greeting.

Lines 93–131

The hostess engages Hal on her behalf in the quarrel. Notice how Hal stays slightly aloof, playing judge, not getting involved until his own name is dragged in.

Depending on how you've viewed Hal throughout the play, you could say that he's indulging in one last merry debate before he goes off to war, or he's acting like the newly reformed heir to the crown, cold and conceited, angry with Falstaff for trying to trick an honest woman.

Lines 132–213

This segment of the scene mirrors Hal's confrontation with Falstaff over the "incomprehensible lies" in Act II, Scene iv.

Falstaff is once again betrayed by his friends, who accuse him of slandering the Prince of Wales. The hostess tells Hal that Falstaff claimed Hal owed him 1000 pounds and threatened repeatedly to cudgel him if he said the ring was worthless. This may be another version of the slander scene between King Henry and Hotspur in Act I, Scene ii. Remember that they accused each other of slander during an argument that was based mainly on Henry's unpaid debts.

Hal manipulates Falstaff into having either to admit he's a liar or to carry out his threat to cudgel Hal. Falstaff uses the same escape route he used in Act II, Scene iv: swearing he dared Hal only as he is a friend, not as he is a true prince. Hal attacks Falstaff for lying, nevertheless, in much the same way as he did before, with images of obesity, dishonesty, and disrespect.

Hal's anger (real or fake) is so sweeping that he finds himself admitting to the pickpocketing without realizing it:

> . . . Why . . . if there were anything in thy pocket but tavern reckonings, memorandums of bawdy houses, and one poor pennyworth of sugar candy . . . if thy pocket were enriched with any other injuries but these, I am a villain.

For once Falstaff really has Hal trapped. He delivers his challenge slowly, relishing his victory: "You confess then, you picked my pocket?" Hal is so stunned at his own unexpected confession that he can only hang his head and answer, "It appears so by the story."

Falstaff is elated: The true prince has proved to be a false thief after all. He asks Hal for news of the court. Hal admits that he has returned the stolen Gad's Hill money, clearing Falstaff of the charge. Hal's words are almost fatherly. As Falstaff's "good angel," Hal will keep the old knight from coming to too much harm. As a true prince, Hal ensures that justice is still accomplished, despite allowing the thieves to remain free. He has cleared his debts in the tavern and is now ready to assume full princely responsibilities.

Falstaff, still a mischievous thief, promptly asks Hal to rob the king's treasury for him, like a good lad. But Hal isn't listening; his thoughts have returned to the troubles at court where he belongs now. He gives Falstaff charge of the foot soldiers, issues orders to Bardolph, Peto, and Falstaff, and leaves.

Hal's last words in the tavern are in the form of a rhymed couplet, a kind of summarizing tag line that points up his relationship to the rest of the play's action: "The land is burning; Percy stands on high; And either we or they must lower lie." He's now firmly committed to a rivalry with Hotspur.

Falstaff's spirits have returned, now that he sees Hal confidently fighting for the future of England. Happiness makes Falstaff feel like eating, and he calls for the hostess to bring in his breakfast: "Rare words! brave world! Hostess, my breakfast, come. O, I wish this tavern were my drum!"

Falstaff, too, recites a couplet, but his rhyme shows he's committed to adventure, eating, and drinking—just as he was at the beginning of the play.

ACT IV

ACT IV, SCENE I

In the time scheme of Shakespeare's play, the ninth of next month—the time for the rebellion—has arrived. The scene is in the rebels' camp at Shrewsbury. You can hear drums pounding and soldiers marching in the distance.

For a fleeting moment at the opening of this scene the rebel leaders are confident in their rebellion. Hotspur and Worcester, with Douglas, are waiting for their allies to arrive and for the battle to begin.

But instead of reinforcements, a messenger arrives. Northumberland has written to say he's sick, maybe dying, and can't muster an army. Northumberland isn't coming. The warnings in the letter Hotspur received from the unnamed lord in Act II, Scene iii, are starting to come true.

The absence of Northumberland's troops makes a serious hole in the rebel enterprise, and Worcester is worried. Northumberland's letter reminds him that even if they give up the rebellion now, Henry will still have them executed for treason. Hotspur, however, does not mourn his father's illness; he only sees Northumberland's absence as a chance to win even greater glory. If the forces are weakened, he reasons, it will just give more glory to their rebellion, because it's now more dangerous to fight.

Then a rebel spy, Vernon, returns to the camp with reports the rebels hadn't expected: Prince Hal, looking like a young god of war, is leading an army dressed in golden suits of armor. The sight of Hal mounted on his horse has dazzled Vernon. Hal promised a brilliant unmasking in his soliloquy in Act I, Scene ii, and here it is.

Stop it, cries Hotspur to the admiring Vernon, you're making me sick! Hotspur never imagined he'd have to fight against Prince Hal. But he's thrilled that a truly worthy rival has come to Shrewsbury; he can barely wait for Hal to arrive.

Vernon then reveals the news that Glendower's army will be two weeks late, and that the king's army is 30,000 strong. All three rebel leaders realize that they're doomed. But Hotspur shouts recklessly, "Doomsday is near. Die all, die merrily!" Hal's presence will still make the battle worth fighting. Hotspur knows he'll lose the battle, but he's sure he'll kill Prince Hal.

ACT IV, SCENE II

Falstaff's ragged troop of foot soldiers presents a vivid contrast with the description of Hal and his golden warriors.

Marching his soldiers to Shrewsbury, Falstaff takes a few minutes to rest his bulky frame. You see him equipped for battle, but he's still talking about money and drinking, not honor and war.

He's full of his self-importance, and tells you in his soliloquy about the clever trick he played to earn money from the war. First he intentionally recruited 150 cowards who he knew could afford to bribe their way out of military service, and pocketed the bribe money for himself. Then he recruited another 150 men—debtors, mostly, but also the kinds of men you've seen before in the play: unemployed servants (like Bardolph), gentlemen who have no inheritance and no trade (like Poins), drawers who've broken their contracts (like Francis), and innkeepers (like Robin Ostler, whose business was failing). The new recruits are ragged and starving, like scarecrows.

As Prince Hal and another general, Westmoreland, happen to pass Falstaff in the road, they both express shock and alarm at the sight of Falstaff's soldiers. Falstaff shrewdly remarks that beggars will fill a mass grave as well as any men. His joke (which people rarely think funny) totally undercuts Hal and Hotspur's view of battle as a noble meeting ground where honor is won. Falstaff points out the true nature of war—men die, no matter why they're fighting.

Hal is thoroughly disgusted with his old companion's attitude, and orders him to march quickly to Shrewsbury, where the king's army is waiting. As Hal and Westmoreland leave, Falstaff expresses his own view of what's important in life: not duty, loyalty, and courage, but good food and good friends, shared in safe surroundings.

At this moment you may sympathize most with Falstaff's realistic, practical view of life. But remember who he is—a fat drunkard and a failure. Hal may seem callous, cold, and deluded by abstract ideals, but at least he is an effective leader, and has discipline and self-control. Shakespeare doesn't expect you to take one side or the other, but he does want you to see that there are many ways to view life, all of which have some value.

ACT IV, SCENE III

Lines 1–35

It's the night before the battle of Shrewsbury, and the rebel leaders are quarreling over when to start their attack on the king's forces. Hotspur and Douglas, renowned for their courage, want to attack that very night; Worcester and Vernon, more cautious, are trying to persuade them to wait until daylight. They accuse each other of cowardice and defend their honors as best as they can. Underneath, however, you may sense their fear, and possibly their wish to call off the campaign.

Lines 36–58

A trumpet sounds, and Sir Walter Blunt rides up. The rebels quickly stop arguing to present a united front before the king's messenger.

Blunt states the rebels' legal position—they stand "out of limit and true rule . . . against anointed majesty." (Notice the similarity of this observation to Falstaff's remarks on his girth in Act III, Scene iii. The fat knight also stands outside all social and political limits.)

NOTE: Blunt is raising one of the central moral and political questions of the play: Is it ever right to rebel against a king? Shakespeare's audience would have said that rebellion against a crowned king is always a grave sin. But what if the king is also a tyrant, or a usurper? Do the same moral attitudes apply?

King Henry was a traitor against the rightful king of England, Richard II. The men who fought with Henry against Richard now fight against Henry. If a thief takes a crown from another thief, has any crime been committed? Or has a form of rough justice triumphed, one thief punishing another? If these questions sound familiar, it's because you considered them in Act II, Scene ii, when Prince Hal robbed Falstaff. Try to apply the answers you gave to Prince Hal's moral dilemma here. Do you still think they fit?

Blunt, in the name of the king, asks the rebels to state their grievances. He delivers an offer from Henry of pardon and safety if they surrender now.

Lines 59–96

Hotspur steps forward to speak for the rebels. His first words are directed at Henry's habit of breaking promises: 'The King is kind, and well we know the King/Knows at what time to promise, when to pay.' If Henry has broken promises to them before, why should he keep this one? Hotspur implies.

Hotspur recites yet another history of the events that led up to the crowning of Henry. All through the play, you've heard hints and fragments of information about Henry's political campaign. But now, just before the battle, Shakespeare presents the evidence *against* the king, like a skillful prosecutor summarizing a case before a jury.

From the beginning of his speech Hotspur describes Henry as a criminal, "a poor unminded outlaw sneaking home." In Hotspur's version of history his father Northumberland was Henry's campaign manager, who led the rest of the country in supporting Henry. Hotspur describes how Henry calculated each step up the ladder of political success, taking opportunities as he found them and turning them into political platforms, all the time seeming to care only about the country's problems. Hotspur is convinced that Henry was after power for his own use.

In Act III, Scene ii, you heard Henry's version of this story. He, too, sees himself as a clever politician, one who is able to win popular support. But Henry didn't tell you all the political events in his campaign. Here, Hotspur is cataloguing some of the worst deeds. At this late moment perhaps Shakespeare is showing you that there are no clearcut heros or villains in this fight. In the middle of war it's sometimes hard to tell which side is "right."

Lines 97–122

Hotspur's history of Henry's crimes against the commonwealth stops with the deposition and murder of Richard. He continues with a list of personal grievances, which are the true reasons for the rebellion. Everything Hotspur lists, you saw happen in Act I, Scene iii. There it seemed that the Percies were contriving a series of challenges to Henry's authority and then accusing the king of acting unreasonably, so they would have grounds for rebellion. But from Hotspur's account here, it does sound like their grievances are very plausible. Think about the accounts of current events you hear on the news. Most of you probably accept these as true. But in this play you've seen events twisted, represented differently to support different factions' political goals. How does this make you feel about what you hear or read in the news?

At the end of his list of grievances Hotspur asks Blunt to bring them some guarantee of safety if they surrender, and Blunt goes back to the royal camp to obtain it. Does this mean that Hotspur is thinking about surrendering, after all his talk about honor? It's a surprising possibility, but we'll never find out, because he won't be given the chance to surrender,— as you'll see in Act V.

ACT IV, SCENE IV

This brief scene gives the illusion of time passing while Blunt is carrying the rebels' answer back to Henry. Like the carrier scene in Act II, this one provides a commentary on the action about to begin.

You're in the Archbishop of York's palace, where a very worried York is sending messages posthaste to the other rebel leaders.

You learn that the king's army outnumbers the rebel army three to one.

NOTE: Think about Falstaff's similar predicament at Gad's Hill: He was outnumbered two to one by the men in buckram. In the face of such overwhelming odds Falstaff chose to turn and run. Faced with even greater odds, however, Hotspur will stand and fight. It's one measure of the differences between these two characters. You have to decide which man you think uses the best strategy.

You also learn that Glendower has refused to show up at Shrewsbury, convinced by prophecies that he shouldn't join in. Mortimer isn't coming to claim his inheritance, either. Could it be that Glendower really knows the outcome of the battle? Or is he merely playing a political game, still annoyed by Hotspur's rude behavior when he was a guest in his house? Either way, you have a growing sense that the rebels' alliance is falling apart.

ACT V

ACT V, SCENE I

On the morning before a civil war, the sun looks bloody and the winds howl ominously. Nature unleashes her fury when a country tears itself apart.

Lines 1–30

In the king's camp Henry, Hal, Prince John, Blunt, and Falstaff assemble to meet with the rebel's emissary, Worcester. A trumpet sounds, and Worcester arrives to answer the king's offer of pardon.

Henry chides Worcester amiably, like an old friend. Worcester agrees that there are better ways he could spend his declining years, but the rebellion could not be avoided. Falstaff jokes cynically that Worcester found rebellion the way you might find a penny in the street while walking (in Elizabethan terms, Worcester found a crown in his path and took it). Hal tells Falstaff to be quiet. The old knight has already shown how absurd Worcester's defense is, but you can also see how out of place Falstaff's roguish wit is when serious matters are being discussed.

Lines 31–83

Now Worcester tells you his version of Henry's political campaign. Rather than sound angry, Worcester manages to sound sad that rebellion was forced on him. Worcester paints Henry more as a victim of time and circumstance than as the self-seeking politician of Hotspur's speech. Worcester says Henry was swept into kingship on a "flood of greatness" and "a swarm of advantages." He drew support from the people—with the Percies' help—but after he assumed his full power, Worcester explains, they were afraid of being swallowed by the new king. Remember Worcester's warning to Henry that the Percies were the true power behind the crown, who brought him to his "portly" greatness (Act I, Scene iii, line 13)? Now he talks about Henry's "bulk" of power. Again, you may think of Falstaff and his contrast with the king.

The main part of Worcester's grievances, though, stems from the broken promises Henry made to the Percies before he became a candidate for kingship. The rebellion, therefore, Worcester claims, was caused by Henry himself, by his "unkind usage, dangerous countenance,/And violation of all faith and troth." Worcester doesn't even mention the deposition. Perhaps he's clever enough to see that he shouldn't accuse Henry of being a traitor when he is hoping to overthrow a king himself.

Lines 84–116

Prince Hal's manner so far in this scene has been detached and critical (as it so often was in the tavern). Now he cuts short the king and Worcester's argument, by offering himself in hand-to-hand combat against Hotspur. Hal offers himself humbly as a "truant" to knighthood, against the man he calls the greatest knight of his time. The odds sound much better for Hotspur this way.

But Hal wouldn't suggest this fight if he didn't think he could win. You've seen before how carefully he reckons his chances before launching any action. You've already learned that he isn't interested in winning honor for its own sake, but intends to force Hotspur to render up every glory. This must be another of Hal's calculated moves in his reformation plan.

Henry is too proud of his son and heir (at last!) to risk losing him. He's seen proof of Hal's diplomatic skill just now, but he knows nothing yet of the young man's military abilities. Henry refuses to let Hal fight

Hotspur, and earnestly entreats Worcester to recon-
sider the offer of pardon, to heal the breach and make
everyone friends again. These optimistic lines seem a
little forced, though. Notice that Henry follows them
with a stern warning of punishment if the rebels insist
on a battle.

Lines 117–122

Worcester departs without another word. The king
and Hal agree that Hotspur and Douglas are too
proud and confident ever to agree to surrender, and
so they begin preparations for battle. Henry goes off
to war, praying for God's help, "as our cause is
just."

These words are ironic, coming from a man whose
list of political crimes you've just heard twice. Yet
Henry is the king, and if order is to be maintained,
any rebellion must be regarded as illegal and sinful.

Lines 123–128

As Hal starts to leave, Falstaff holds him back to ask
for protection in the battle, to prove that they're still
friends.

Hal, however, counsels Falstaff to say his prayers,
and reminds the old man that he owes God his final
reckoning—death. The actor playing Hal might say
these words with bitterness, or with a joking tone, or
with an air of preoccupation, his thoughts already on
the battle. Whichever way he speaks to Falstaff,
though, Hal goes off to join his father, leaving Falstaff
alone before a great battle. The old knight is horseless
as well. His circumstances are just as they were at the
beginning of the Gad's Hill robbery.

Lines 129–143

This time, though, Falstaff doesn't roar for Hal to
come back. He turns Hal's cynical words about death
around; if that's a debt he owes God, then he can put

off paying it. You've seen how much Falstaff dislikes paying his bills; the thought of paying God for his life must seem like the worst reckoning of all. I won't call God, decides Falstaff, if he doesn't call me.

Having thus talked himself into some kind of courage, Falstaff starts to walk off to war. "Honor pricks me on," he announces confidently. But then he stops, thinks, turns around, and has a series of second thoughts.

He wonders if honor is something worth dying for, and proceeds to argue with himself (since no one else is around) over the practical advantages of fighting for honor.

> Can honor set a leg? No. Or an arm? No. . . . What is honor? A word. What is that word honor? . . . Air—a trim reckoning! Who hath it? He that died a Wednesday. Doth he feel it? No. . . . But will it not live with the living? No. Why? Detraction will not suffer it. Therefore I'll none of it. . . .

Honor can give Falstaff neither life nor fame; it won't help him live through a battle or live forever in reputation. The battle Falstaff is about to risk his life in is being fought for honor—and he doubts very much that that's worth dying for.

Some readers say Falstaff's catechism on honor is his way of rationalizing being a coward. Other readers see it as a realistic, if cynical, look at the fortunes of war.

NOTE: If you compare Falstaff's and Hotspur's views of honor, you'll understand the two men's relationship for the rest of the play. To Hotspur, honor is more important than life itself, and the pursuit of honor drives him to his death. He stands for image and ideals. Falstaff hacks away at the meaning of honor until he's reduced it to a puff of air, a word. The only honor worth having is life. Falstaff is physical, realistic, vivid, contradictory—a slice of life.

ACT V, SCENE II

In this scene the rebels deceive each other.

Lines 1–27

In most stage productions of this play the audience sees the battle starting now. Trumpets are blaring, drums are beating; soldiers are fastening helmets, checking their weapons, giving and taking orders.

Worcester tells Vernon not even to tell Hotspur of the king's "liberal and kind" offer for peace. Worcester doesn't trust the king to keep his word; once you're a traitor, he points out, you'll always be regarded as a traitor, so there's no way we can really go back to our former position at court. Hotspur, however, is likely to escape the king's punishment, Worcester adds, because we'll be blamed for misleading and corrupting him. "We did train him on," sighs the old politician, and we "shall pay for all." Unlike Prince Hal, Hotspur couldn't see that his elder companions were misleading him. Hal rejected Falstaff, but Hotspur joined Worcester and Northumberland. His downfall thus began at just about the same time as Hal's reformation.

Lines 28–43

Hotspur and Douglas enter together to discover what happened between Worcester and King Henry. Notice that the rebel leaders are still split into two factions, divided by different levels of courage and politics. Their internal dissension is in contrast to the solid front on the king's side.

Worcester lies, telling Hotspur that "There is no seeming mercy in the King." Douglas is sent to find Westmoreland, to deliver the rebels' challenge.

Lines 44–72

Douglas returns almost immediately with a frantic call to arms. Now that the war has been officially declared, Worcester feels it's safe to tell Hotspur about Hal's challenge to fight him in single combat. Hotspur's reaction exactly parallels Hal's offer: Both young men wish they could fight this war alone, and together.

Vernon describes Hal's challenge in glowing terms, and speaks of Hal's amazing transformation:

> If he outlive the envy of this day,
> England did never owe so sweet a hope,
> So much misconstrued in his wantonness.

Nobody on stage in this scene wants to hear this. The battle preparations stop, and no one else speaks. Hal has redeemed his bad reputation—exactly as he said he would.

NOTE: Everyone in Shakespeare's audience knew what would happen next—Hal would kill Hotspur in hand-to-hand combat. Hal appears here like the sudden blaze of a comet, lighting up the dark sky of rebellion. It's an omen: a good one for England and a poor one for Hotspur. It's a mirror that he could look into and see his own death.

Lines 73–104

Yet Hotspur buoyantly teases Vernon for being "enamored" of Hal's new image, and promises to crush Hal by hugging him—in a soldier's death-grip

embrace. Hotspur turns to his soldiers and gives them
a rousing pep talk. But a messenger arrives; Hotspur
ignores him. He keeps talking boldly about their
future glory, whether they win or lose, live or die. A
second messenger arrives, announcing that the king's
army is coming. Hotspur and his soldiers on stage are
locked together in an embrace of soldierly commit-
ment, though the odds against their winning are
impossibly high. The trumpets play. Before the military tattoo is over, the stage is left empty.

ACT V, SCENE III

During the battle of Shrewsbury, all the major
themes are brought together, and focus on the figure
of Prince Hal.

Lines 1–33

Henry enters with his army. They take up battle
positions for an attack. At the sound of a trumpet,
they rush noisily into battle (offstage).

NOTE: The king's shrewd tactic is to send lords
dressed in his royal colors into battle. Douglas will kill
these "kings" one by one, until he finally meets the
real king of England. These "counterfeit" kings may
symbolize all the claimants for the crown in the play,
or they may be signs that Henry is as much of a coward as Falstaff, disguising his fears with mighty
images. It is indeed ironic that Henry, the royal
impostor, should send royal impostors into battle to
defend his crown.

Lines 34–43

Falstaff, running as fast as he can, stumbles over
one of the dead "counterfeits," Sir Walter Blunt.
"There's honor for you! Here's no vanity!" he cries.

Blunt's lifeless body perfectly illustrates Falstaff's conception of honor.

Falstaff willingly has led his ragamuffin soldiers into wholesale slaughter: not even three of them are left alive. His pathetic army, though comical, serves as an ironic commentary on Henry's royal counterfeits. Both the foot soldiers and the disguised noblemen now lie in the mud. Yet Falstaff is alive, against great odds.

Lines 44–61

When he hears someone coming near, Falstaff looks for a hiding place. He's relieved to discover it's no one fiercer than Prince Hal. Falstaff tells him a monstrous lie, that he's done Hal a great favor and killed Hotspur. Hal calls Falstaff a liar and asks to borrow his sword. Falstaff gives Hal a bottle of sack instead. But Hal furiously throws the bottle at Falstaff; the middle of a battlefield is no place for jokes. This episode shows Hal as a dedicated soldier—and it shows Falstaff's continued resistance to the honor of war.

Lines 62–67

Alone, Falstaff makes a bargain with himself to fight Hotspur—if their paths should happen to cross. He takes another look at dead Blunt, and shudders. "Give me life," he declares. If he can't live, he knows he'll have honor in his death, but he doesn't particularly want to pursue that.

ACT V, SCENE IV

Lines 1–25

The royal father and sons meet on the edge of the battlefield. Hal is badly wounded but refuses to rest. He advises Henry to return to the fighting, lest the army think he's dead and lose heart.

NOTE: When Henry returned from exile and began his campaign to become king, King Richard II was in Ireland, losing a war. His return to England was delayed by bad weather, and many people thought he was dead. That was one of the reasons Henry had so little trouble taking the crown. The fact that Henry returns to the battle at Shrewsbury is a clue that, unlike Richard, he will win and keep his crown.

Here you see Hal in the garment of blood he promised to put on in Act III, Scene ii. He's proving to be a brave soldier and continues to brush off his father's cautious advice. He praises his younger brother like a generous knight and scorns his wounds with as much disregard as Hotspur does.

Lines 26-62

The king's army of counterfeit kings seem to pop up everywhere (much like Falstaff's army of imaginary thieves in Act II, Scene iv). When Douglas faces Henry and challenges Henry's identity, he voices one of the play's central questions: Who is the real king?

Douglas remains skeptical, although he admits that this man bears himself like a king. So, you know, did Falstaff when he was play-acting in the tavern. Both Henry and Falstaff steal crowns and both manage to act like kings. Does acting like a king entitle a man to rule? Hotspur is called the "king of honor" and is Henry's ideal of an heir. Mortimer is Richard's designated heir. Each has a claim to the crown, but does either of them deserve to be king?

Whether or not Douglas is convinced that he is indeed standing before the true king, he fights Henry, an older and weaker man, to the ground. Henry is about to be robbed of his life and his crown, when Prince Hal arrives on the scene. He announces his identity to Douglas: "It is the Prince of Wales that threatens thee,/Who never promiseth but he means to pay." Douglas does not doubt Hal's word or his ability with a sword. Henry may be vulnerable, but his son is not. After fighting with Hal, Douglas flees.

The true prince rescues his father and restores his crown to him. (Remember that he restored the treasury "crowns" stolen at Gad's Hill, in Act III, Scene iii.)

Henry praises Hal's behavior and admits that the young man has overturned his father's opinion of him. The king welcomes Hal back into the line of succession. He confesses that he thought Hal wanted him dead. Hal's reply to his father is bitter but honest; it's dangerous to listen to rumors, he says. If my bad reputation had been real, father, you would now be dead. Notice how realistic their reconciliation is. It takes a long time for people to learn to trust each other again after a long estrangement. There's no sudden, magical reunion here.

Lines 63–117

As the king limps away to return to battle, Hotspur appears before Hal. Hotspur has come to steal Hal's title, his claim to the crown. Hal now has a chance to take away Hotspur's honors, with which he intends to "make a garland for my head"—a crown of honor.

Notice that the very minute Hal becomes Hotspur's equal in Henry's eyes, Hotspur arrives to challenge him. Now that they are equal at last, only one of them can live: "England cannot brook a double reign/Of Harry Percy and the Prince of Wales," Hal warns Hotspur.

As the rival princes fight, Falstaff enters and stands nearby, cheering Hal on from the sidelines just as he cheered on the thieves at Gad's Hill.

Douglas reenters, and finding no more kings to fight, he challenges Sir John Falstaff (who has, after all, looked like a king before in this play). The old knight fights as long as he sees reason—and then falls down, pretending to die. (Sometimes on stage, the actor playing Falstaff falls down before Douglas strikes even one blow.) Falstaff moans as though in his death agonies. Douglas comes closer to inspect his dying foe. Falstaff suddenly lies very still, pretending to be dead. Douglas shrugs and moves off, looking for better opponents.

At the very moment Falstaff feigns death, on another part of the stage Hal mortally wounds Hotspur. As Hotspur dies, he mourns the loss of his honor more than the loss of his life. To the end, he remains consistently the "King of honor."

NOTE: Dying, Hotspur sees himself as "life's fool," but some readers say that Hotspur is honor's fool. Hotspur's view of himself is romantic and tragic. Falstaff might say that his loss of life is ridiculous. Why choose to be food for worms when there are so many good things in life?

Hal mourns the dead Hotspur as he would a brother. He does not steal Hotspur's honor, after all, but generously allows Hotspur to "take thy praise with thee to heaven." Just as he returned the stolen crowns and his father's crown, so Hal now restores Hotspur's crown of honor. Hal tenderly covers Hotspur's mangled face with a few feathers plucked from his helmet. This noble gesture shows how well Hal deserves his own title, the "king of courtesy."

As Hal rises from bending over Hotspur's body, he sees Falstaff lying "dead." Having just spoken a eulogy over Hotspur, now he speaks one over Falstaff. Hal treated Hotspur like a prince, but he treats his old friend with a more familiar, joking tone:

> Poor Jack, farewell!
> I could have better spared a better man.
> O, I should have a heavy miss of thee
> If I were much in love with vanity.

"Vanity" is empty boasting, Falstaff's brand of honor, which Hal has now rejected. In spite of himself, Hal is sorry to lose a good friend, but he won't miss his frivolity. Hal promises to pay for Falstaff's funeral, to have him emboweled for posterity.

On stage, Hal would be now standing between his two models, Hotspur and Falstaff: between virtue and vice, courage and cowardice, spirit and sensuality, rebel and thief. He looks at both bodies and walks away.

Lines 118–136

Falstaff may want to lose weight but disemboweling wasn't what he had in mind. He gets to his feet as quickly as possible and proceeds to rationalize his counterfeit death as "the true and perfect image of life." You might say that the dead Hotspur is the true and perfect image of honor. To Falstaff, however, a better honor is "discretion," knowing when to run for one's life.

Falstaff sees Hotspur's dead body, and his cynical, practical view immediately transforms the corpse's value. Falstaff sees it as a chance to steal some glory. He looks around to make sure no one is watching, stabs Hotspur in the thigh, and throws the corpse over his shoulders like a sack of potatoes.

Lines 137-174

As Falstaff lugs away Hotspur, Hal and John return to attend to the bodies. They watch Falstaff struggle, fascinated. Hal can't believe his eyes, but Falstaff assures them he is very much alive. He tosses Hotspur to the ground with a mock humility, and claims whatever reward is due.

Falstaff is claiming the reward for killing the greatest knight as well as the king's worst enemy. Hal stands dumbfounded while Falstaff spins another web of monstrous lies about his duel with Hotspur. Falstaff accuses Hal of lying and boasts that he and Hotspur fought for an hour before he wounded Hotspur. Falstaff never actually says he killed Hotspur, but implies it with great bravado:

> If I may be believed, so; if not, let them that should
> reward valor bear the sin upon their own heads.

Falstaff has turned Hotspur's beloved ideal of military glory into a quest for tangible rewards, for titles, wealth, and social status. These are the commodities Hal has just rejected, the elements of honor he doesn't need.

To his credit, Hal takes the whole thing as a joke, and promises to see how much he can get for Falstaff as a reward. Can you imagine Hotspur doing the same? Hal's honor is proving to be not only a sense of humility with the people of England, but also a sense of security that needs no outward display. Perhaps you've known people like this, who don't have to be conceited about their good qualities. Do you think they make good leaders?

As the trumpet sounds the retreat, Hal and John go to survey the field. You learn that the king's army has won.

With Hotspur's body flung across his back, Falstaff goes off, promising to repent, lose weight, stop drinking, and live modestly, "as a nobleman should do." When Falstaff reappears in *Henry IV, Part 2*, Hal will have procured him a pension; Falstaff will be dressed lavishly and living off a fake reputation as a great military hero.

ACT V, SCENE V

You can see the victory at Shrewsbury as a sign that King Henry has won the right to rule England. He has also ensured the rightful succession of the crown, by restoring Prince Hal to favor. But because Henry's a usurper, rebels will grow like Hydra's heads; there are still threats to his kingdom. King Henry therefore divides his triumphant army in two, to march against Northumberland and York, Glendower and Mortimer. The play ends as it began, with civil uprisings and bloodshed.

Notice that Henry is still not a perfect king. He exercises justice arbitrarily; he condemns Worcester and Vernon to death but allows Prince Hal to free Douglas. But unlike his behavior in Act I, Scene i, Henry seems here to be acting with a firm control over the destinies of his people, and trusts his son to administer justice.

Hal is definitely emerging as a model leader. His attitude toward prisoners of war contrasts with Hotspur's in Act I. Hotspur treated his "honorable spoil" as political pawns, but Hal graciously allows his brother John to free his "honorable bounty" Douglas unconditionally. The battle of Shrewsbury has taught Hal "to cherish such high deeds,/Even in the bosom of our adversaries." As a true prince, Hal shows generosity to his enemies and courtesy to the court. As a good politician, Hal values Douglas' military skill—a grateful Scottish general would be a powerful asset to an English king—and bends the laws against treason in order to gain a potential ally.

Royal grace mixes equally with shrewd political ability in the character of Prince Hal. This balance of leadership qualities will help him become England's great hero-king, Henry V. But that's another play.

A STEP BEYOND

Tests and Answers

TESTS

Test 1

1. Shakespeare's principal source for this play   _____
   was
   A. Geoffrey of Monmouth's *Historia Regnum Brittaniae*
   B. Holinshed's *Chronicles*
   C. Belleforest's *Histoires Tragiques*

2. At the time Henry IV learned of the rebellion,   _____
   he had been planning
   A. his own invasion of France
   B. to turn his throne over to the Prince of Wales
   C. to undertake an expedition to the Holy Land

3. King Henry IV was buoyed over the   _____
   A. conquest of the Scots by Hotspur
   B. ransom of Edmund Mortimer
   C. the surrender of Owen Glendower

4. When Henry is informed of Hotspur's   _____
   performance, he
   A. belittles the young man's achievement
   B. wishes that his own son were as brave
   C. awards him the title of Earl of Northumberland

5. Prince Hal calls Falstaff: _____
     I. an old lad of the castle
     II. a purple-headed malt worm
     III. a fat-kidneyed rascal
  A. I and II only
  B. I and III only
  C. II and III only

6. The angry Henry closes his ears to the _____
mention of the name of
  A. the Earl of Westmoreland
  B. the Earl of Worcester
  C. Edmund Mortimer

7. In describing Falstaff's movement, Prince Hall _____
says
  A. "Here waddles Sir Beer Barrel"
  B. "He lards the earth as he walks along"
  C. "I have seen daintier elephants"

8. "Thou wilt not utter what thou dost not _____
know" is an explanation for keeping a secret,
given by
  A. Hotspur to Lady Percy
  B. Prince Hal to Falstaff
  C. Falstaff to Mistress Quickly

9. Prince Hal also calls Falstaff _____
     I. bed-presser
     II. horse-back-breaker
     III. huge hill of flesh
  A. I and II only
  B. II and III only
  C. I, II, and III

10. Falstaff tells his lies at the _____
  A. tavern in Eastcheap
  B. Mermaid Tavern on the Bankside
  C. Garter Inn in Windsor

11. What role does honor play in *Henry IV, Part I?*

12. What is the relationship between the worlds of the court and the tavern in the play?

13. How does Shakespeare guide your feelings about the rebels?

14. Trace one of the major imagery patterns (counterfeiting, disorder, or horsemanship) through the play.

15. Discuss the education of Prince Hal.

Test 2

1. The best praise for Falstaff comes from _____
   A. Prince Hal—when he counters his father's criticism
   B. Falstaff—when he plays the role of King Henry
   C. Poins and Gadshill—when they toast their drinking partner

2. Rhyming couplets such as away/delay, _____ short/sport, and come/drum generally signify
   A. a nobleman's speech
   B. the end of an act
   C. a line of iambic tetrameter

3. The rebels show their confidence by _____
   A. dividing up the map of England
   B. demanding that King Henry surrender
   C. challenging the royal army at Shrewsbury

4. A critical moment in the play comes when _____
   Prince Hal
   A. entrusts Falstaff with the command of foot soldiers
   B. swears to be worthy of his name

    C. offers to meet Owen Glendower in single combat

5. "Harry to Harry shall, hot horse to horse, _____ Meet and ne'er part till one drop down a corse" is spoken by
   A. Prince Hal
   B. Hotspur
   C. Archibald, Earl of Douglas

6. Bad news for the rebels comes with the _____
   A. Archbishop's proclamation of their excommunication
   B. desertion of 3000 soldiers
   C. absence of Northumberland and Glendower

7. King Henry seeks to avoid bloodshed by _____
   A. asking Hotspur and Douglas to accept a truce
   B. offering a full pardon to the rebels if they disperse
   C. offering to redress the rebels' grievances expeditiously

8. The bloody battle in Act V was precipitated _____ by
   A. Worcester's lie
   B. Hotspur's arrogance
   C. Douglas' duplicity

9. In the heat of the battle, Prince Hal _____
       I. slays Douglas, Vernon, and Worcester
       II. kills Hotspur
       III. saves his father's life
   A. I and II only
   B. II and III only
   C. I and III only

10. "Ill-weaved ambition, how much art thou _____ shrunk!" is said by
    A. Hal to Hotspur's body
    B. King Henry to Lord Douglas
    C. Hal to the cowardly Falstaff

11. Discuss how Hotspur and Falstaff serve as models for Prince Hal.

12. What is the relationship between King Henry and Falstaff?

13. Compare the various speeches on Henry's usurpation of the crown.

14. Discuss the motives for the Percy rebellion.

ANSWERS

Test 1

1. B	2. C	3. A	4. B	5. B	6. C
7. B	8. A	9. C	10. A		

11. *Honor* is one of the most frequently occurring words in the play. Focus on three characters—most likely Hotspur, Falstaff, and Prince Hal—and discuss what honor means to each. Pay particular attention to: Hotspur's reactions in Act I, Scene iii, and throughout Act IV; to Falstaff's speeches on honor in Act V; and to Prince Hal's discussion of the drawers in Act II, Scene iv and his promises to King Henry in Act III, Scene ii. Then you could focus on the battle of Shrewsbury, where the honor of all three characters is tested. Explain how this is done, and what you learn about the characters as a result. Talk about how the pursuit or avoidance of honor guides the characters' action. In your summing up, discuss the relationship between kingship and honor, and between politics and honor. How does Shakespeare's exploration of the many definitions of honor affect your interpretation of the plot?

12.   Start by describing each world separately. Who lives in the court, and who in the tavern? Talk about the fact that only Prince Hal lives in both, and why. What are the characters' professions and interests? How do they talk?

Then discuss the relationship between court and tavern. What is common to both worlds? (How are rebellion and robbery related in the play?)

What is different about the two worlds? Talk about Shakespeare's episodic structure and its series of contrasts and comparisons. Look at the sequence of scenes, and their nature or character. Find images common to both worlds, like crowns, stealing, and counterfeiting. Discuss how the imagery relates the two worlds. How are the common themes of rebellion, education, and authority applied to the situations in each world?

13.   First identify the Percies as King Henry's former allies. Describe their different versions of Henry's rise to power (look at the speeches of Hotspur and Worcester on the subject). What reasons do they give for the rebellion, and how are you meant to feel about these reasons? Then look briefly at each member of the family. What kind of role does Northumberland, for instance, play in the conspiracy? What about Worcester?

List the Percies' allies, and explain why they were chosen to join the conspiracy.

As soon as the conspiracy is formed, it begins to fall apart. Describe how Shakespeare makes you feel uneasy about the nature of the conspirators, and especially as the battle nears. Look at Hotspur's reaction to the unnamed lord's letter in Act II, Scene iii; the scene in Glendower's castle, where the rebels divide up England and quarrel among themselves; and the scene where only Hotspur, Worcester, and Douglas show up at Shrewsbury. Why do the other rebels (Northumberland, Glendower, and Mortimer) refuse to come? Do you think they ever really intended to show up?

Look at Worcester's reaction to King Henry's offer for peace. Why does Worcester refuse to tell Hotspur about it? What effect does his secrecy have on the outcome of the play?

After the battle, Worcester and Vernon are executed, Hotspur is dead, and Douglas is allowed to go free. Has justice been served? Are the rebels treated fairly by the king? by Hal?

14. *Counterfeiting:* Define the meaning of counterfeiting, first as minting a false currency and then as acting a role instead of being the person you really are. What is the relationship between Henry's usurped crown (a counterfeit kingship) and the stolen crowns of the thieves?

There are many variations of the image of counterfeiting in the play. Counterfeit crowns, for example, appear as the usurped crown, as stolen crowns; false kings, theatrical kings, imaginary armies, disguised armies. Cracked crowns are also broken heads (in the inn-yard scene of Act II, Scene i). Falstaff counterfeits death at Shrewsbury.

Finally, discuss how the nature of counterfeiting is a theme of the play.

Disorder: Traditionally the images of disease and disorder in the play have been seen as a moral commentary on the state of the kingdom. But you may also chose to see these images as descriptions of the natural condition of man in society, particularly in a monarchy where the nobles feud for power.

Disorder takes the form of broken promises (King Henry), civil war (both in Act I, Scene i and at Shrewsbury), the life in the tavern (pay particular attention to Falstaff's attempts to turn Prince Hal into a criminal king), in a son's disobedience to his father (both Hal and Hotspur), and in the emblems of anarchy discussed in the inn-yard scene.

Disease images also fill the play. Falstaff is obese (describe him at Gad's Hill); Northumberland's illness breeds sickness in the rebels' army; King Henry is nervous and anxious; and before the battle at Shrewsbury, the sun and wind play havoc, reflecting the disease in men who rebel against the state.

Horsemanship: One theme of the play is chivalry—knights in armor fighting on horseback. Hotspur loves riding, but Falstaff is forced to walk, both at Gad's Hill and at Shrewsbury. Prince Hal appears riding to Shrewsbury like a young god of war. Discuss how these three characters' attitudes toward horses and riding reflect their personalities and moral positions in the play.

Horses are also a symbol of vitality. Their presence in this play is one way Shakespeare describes the energy unleashed by the various civil disorders. Although horses can't be brought on stage, describe how Shakespeare makes you hear their hooves pounding (the messengers arriving and departing throughout, armies approaching) through the kingdom. Discuss how the racing and charging of horses described in the imagery creates an impression of haste, and of how time is compressed dramatically through this device.

15. Set up your answer by describing what Hal is like at the beginning of the play, and then what he has proven himself to be by the end. Talk about the tavern world and what he learns there; then talk about the battle of Shrewsbury and what Hal learns there. What leadership qualities has Hal inherited from his father? What other qualities does he acquire and how might they make him a better king than Henry? Conclude your answer by defining a good leader (as you think Shakespeare defines it) and then discuss how Hal does and does not fit that definition by the end of the play.

Test 2

1. B   2. B   3. A   4. B   5. B   6. C
7. B   8. A   9. B   10. A

11. You can begin your discussion with a description of the theme of "the education of a prince." What is Prince Hal's task in the play? Why is it important to the plot? Look at his conversations with Falstaff, at his soliloquy in Act I, scene ii, and at his description of Hotspur in Act II, scene iv.

Demonstrate how Shakespeare educates Prince Hal by comparing him with Hotspur or contrasting him to Falstaff. For this you will first have to list both Hotspur's and Falstaff's chief traits. How do they feel about honor, loyalty, war, justice, and honesty? What are their qualifications for leadership?

Discuss how Hotspur and Falstaff share some personality traits and contrast vividly in others. How do these features compare with Prince Hal's personality? Does the prince share any of them?

Hotspur and Falstaff represent opposite extremes in the code and conduct of life. You can argue that Prince Hal finds a balance between these two extremes or that he picks and chooses among these attitudes, guided by circumstances.

Finally, explain why Prince Hal acts the way he does. Discuss his personality and his motivations. Do his encounters with Hotspur and Falstaff help or hinder his education in kingship?

12. Begin with a discussion of the nature of authority in the play. Talk about the idea of kingship, and about the relationship between fathers and sons.

Then describe King Henry's character. Talk about his moral position as a usurper and a crowned king. Next describe Falstaff's basic characteristics and discuss his profession as a thief and his function as "king of the tavern." How does this mirroring relationship between these two characters make you feel about each of them?

You could concentrate your discussion by comparing: Henry's yearning to go on a crusade and Falstaff's role as "Monsieur Remorse"; the tavern interview and the court interview with Prince Hal; the robbery of the crown from Richard and the robbery of crowns at Gad's Hill; or the armies of counterfeit kings in the tavern and at Shrewsbury.

13. First, sum up the historical events that led Henry to power, as objectively as you can. Then discuss, in the order they appear in the play, each of the various versions you are told of this story. What is included and what is left out? What does this tell you about the character who is speaking and the situation he's in? For example, Henry conveniently forgets about the debts he owes to the Percies because he needs to justify his usurpation to himself. Hotspur sees Henry as a vile politician who murdered Richard, the "sweet, lovely rose," because Hotspur idealizes the past. Worcester says Henry could not help becoming king because he wants to play down Henry's abilities and emphasize the Percies' role.

In your final paragraph discuss what the effect of these different versions of history is. How do they make the audience feel at each point? How do they relate to the themes of the play?

14. Discuss briefly why each of these allies joined the rebellion. For example, begin with the Percies themselves. Worcester and Northumberland fear that Henry is plotting to murder them for their part in the conspiracy to depose Richard II, and they want a bigger share of his power. They plot to give Hotspur three reasons to fight Henry: they create a situation in which the king is forced to insult Hotspur's sense of personal honor with the Scottish prisoners; they give Hotspur a legal claimant to Richard's throne to champion (Mortimer); and they remind Hotspur that their family honor has been badly tarnished for their part in the deposition of Richard. Hotspur, decides to rebel in order to redeem his honor.

Discuss Glendower, Mortimer, York, and Douglas: What do they hope to gain from the rebellion?

Finally, discuss how this rebellion affects England. Is Henry to blame because he created the political conditions for it to ripen in? How does the rebellion express Shakespeare's view of history? Is the Percies' rebellion just one part of the natural chaos that results from deposing a rightful king? How does the rebellion connect to the other themes of the play—leadership, counterfeiting, fathers and sons?

Term Paper Ideas

1. How are the images of crowns, hanging, or disorder related to Shakespeare's plot? Follow one of these images through the play and discuss how it affects your impression of characters and events.

2. Examine the imagery of counterfeiting and play-acting. How does it work as a comment on kingship and politics?

3. Discuss the qualities a man needs to be a good king? How does Shakespeare explore the nature of kingship?

4. Examine this play as a satire on chivalry and war. Use the characters of Hotspur, the popinjay lord, Falstaff, and Prince Hal as your guides.

5. Consider the presentation of women in the play. Compare Lady Percy with the tavern hostess. How do they act toward Hotspur and Falstaff, respectively? What is Lady Mortimer's function in Act III, Scene i?

6. Compare the carrier scene and the Archbishop of York scene. What are their functions in the play?

7. Compare Hotspur's scene with Lady Percy (Act II, Scene iii) with the scene between Brutus and Portia in Act II, Scene i of *Julius Caesar*.

8. Discuss where you think the center of the play lies. Is it with the rivalry between Hal and Hotspur; with Hal's choice between the worlds represented by Hotspur and Falstaff; or with the consequences of rebellion and crime?

9. Compare Henry IV's character in *Richard II* and *Henry IV*.

10. Even though we no longer have kings who rule absolutely, our world has dictators and tyrants, civil wars, and rising crime rates. Consider whether the problems of a medieval English king have relevance for you today. What lessons can you learn from this play?

11. You can see the play as a story about two rival families. Compare the Percies and the royal family in terms of political motivations and actions, and the relationships between fathers and sons.

12. Examine whether the characters of King Henry, Prince Hal, Hotspur, and Falstaff change and develop during the play. If you think any of them does, which of his character traits change, under what conditions, and to what effect? If the character(s) remain the same from beginning to end, what forms the dramatic interest of the plot?

Further Reading

CRITICAL WORKS

Brown, John Russell. *"Henry IV, Part One,"* in *Shakespeare in Performance*. New York: Harcourt Brace Jovanovich, 1976.

Brooks, Cleanth, and Robert B. Heilman. "Introduction to *Henry IV, Part One,"* in *Understanding Drama*. New York: Rinehart, 1948.

Burgess, Anthony. *Shakespeare*. London: Penguin, 1972.

Chute, Marchette. *An Introduction to Shakespeare*. New York: Dutton, 1951.

Ornstein, Robert. *"Henry IV Part One,"* in *A Kingdom for a Stage*. Cambridge, Mass.: Harvard University Press, 1972.

Prior, Moody E. *The Drama of Power: Studies in Shakespeare's History Plays*. Evanston, Ill.: Northwestern University Press, 1973.

Saccio, Peter. "Henry IV: The King Embattled," in *Shakespeare's English Kings*. New York: Oxford University Press, 1977.

Tillyard, E. M. W. *"Henry IV Part One,"* in *Shakespeare's History Plays*. New York, 1947.

Wilson, John Dover, ed. *Life in Shakespeare's England*. London: Penguin, 1911.

Winny, James. "The Royal Counterfeit," in *The Player King*. London: Chatto & Windus, 1968.

AUTHOR'S OTHER WORKS

Shakespeare wrote 37 plays (38 if you include *The Two Noble Kinsmen*) over a 20-year period, from about 1590 to 1612. It's difficult to determine the exact dates when many were written, but scholars have made the following intelligent guesses about his plays and poems:

Plays

1588–93	The Comedy of Errors
1588–94	Love's Labor's Lost
1590–91	2 Henry VI
1590–91	3 Henry VI
1591–92	1 Henry VI
1592–93	Richard III
1592–94	Titus Andronicus
1593–94	The Taming of the Shrew
1593–95	The Two Gentlemen of Verona
1594–96	Romeo and Juliet
1595	Richard II
1594–96	A Midsummer Night's Dream
1596–97	King John
1596–97	The Merchant of Venice
1597	1 Henry IV
1597–98	2 Henry IV
1598–1600	Much Ado About Nothing
1598–99	Henry V
1599	Julius Caesar
1599–1600	As You Like It
1599–1600	Twelfth Night
1600–01	Hamlet
1597–1601	The Merry Wives of Windsor
1601–02	Troilus and Cressida
1602–04	All's Well That Ends Well
1603–04	Othello
1604	Measure for Measure
1605–06	King Lear
1605–06	Macbeth
1606–07	Antony and Cleopatra
1605–08	Timon of Athens
1607–09	Coriolanus
1608–09	Pericles
1609–10	Cymbeline
1610–11	The Winter's Tale

| 1611–12 | *The Tempest* |
| 1612–13 | *Henry VIII* |

Poems

1592	*Venus and Adonis*
1593–94	*The Rape of Lucrece*
1593–1600	*Sonnets*
1600–01	*The Phoenix and the Turtle*

Glossary of Characters

Archibald, the fourth Earl of Douglas Born 1369, known as "Tyneman" in history. Fought at Shrewsbury, but was captured and kept prisoner until 1408. He later fought with the French against Henry V. He was killed in battle in 1424.

Falstaff, Sir John Fictitious knight and companion of Prince Hal, based probably on Sir John Oldcastle, who was a companion of the real Henry IV's and possibly a friend to Prince Hal. Oldcastle was born in 1378; he was High Sheriff of Herefordshire and became Lord Cobham by marriage in 1409. He fought in France with Henry V, but was accused of heresy and executed in London in 1417.

Glendower, Owen Welsh nobleman, Lord of Glyndwyr, descended from Llewellyn, the last of the Welsh kings. Born 1359, he possibly served as a lawyer at Richard II's court, and was educated in England. Glendower first rebelled against Henry IV over the king's handling of a real estate dispute with one of his neighbors. Defeated at Shrewsbury, he joined with the French against Henry V in 1405. Renowned for his magical abilities. Died in 1415.

King Henry IV Born 1367 at Bolingbroke, Lincolnshire, the eldest son of John of Gaunt, who was Duke of Lancaster and a grandson of King Edward III. Created Duke of Hereford under Richard II, he was then banished by Richard in 1398. He returned to England in 1399 to claim his deceased father's title, but with popular support and the approval of Parliament, became king. He ruled England from 1399–1413, when he died (possibly of leprosy) in a chamber in his palace called Jerusalem.

Henry, Prince of Wales Born 1387 at Monmouth, Wales. The eldest son of King Henry IV, Prince Hal became King Henry V after his father's death in 1413. He conquered

France and married the French king's daughter, Katherine. He died in France in 1422, leaving a young child Henry VI, on the throne.

John of Gaunt Born 1340, third son of King Edward III. His name derives from his birthplace, Ghent, in Flanders. He was created Earl of Richmond in 1342; Duke of Lancaster in 1361; Duke of Aquitaine in 1390. Died in 1399.

John, Duke of Lancaster Born 1389, third son of Henry IV. He captured leaders of the northern rebellion and had them executed after promising amnesty. He became Regent of France under King Henry V; later he conquered Orleans and Rouen, where he died in 1435.

Mortimer, Edmund, Fifth Earl of March Born 1391, he was the heir to his father's claim to the throne after 1398, but he was a friend to Henry V. He died of the plague in 1425.

Mortimer, Roger, Fourth Earl of March Born 1374, he was heir designate to Richard II's crown. He died in 1398.

Percy, Henry, Duke of Northumberland Born 1342, he was the head of the most powerful baronial family in England. Died in 1408.

Percy, Henry, known as Hotspur Born 1364, he was the son of Northumberland and a nephew of Worcester. He died in 1403 at the battle of Shrewsbury, by an unknown hand. He was married to Elizabeth Mortimer, daughter of the third Earl of March.

Percy, Thomas, Earl of Worcester Born 1342, he was captured and executed at Shrewsbury, 1403.

King Richard II Born 1366, son of the Prince of Wales, Edward, the Black Prince. When Edward III died (after his son and heir, the Black Prince), Richard assumed the crown at age eleven. John of Gaunt was made Protector of the realm until Richard was twenty years old. Richard suppressed Wat Tyler's rebellion in 1381. He was married twice: in 1382 to Anne of Bohemia, who died in 1394; in 1396 to Isabella of France, (who was only eight years old), for political reasons. Also called Richard of Bordeaux, he was the eighth Plantagenet king. He was deposed and died in mysterious circumstances, 1399–1400.

The Critics

On King Henry IV

The one serious flaw in a brilliantly arranged usurpation was Henry's dependence on powerful men for the support necessary to take the crown from Richard, while at the same time seeking to maintain the independence and inherent power of the office.

> —*Moody E. Prior*, The Drama of Power, 1973

On Prince Hal

The prince, who is the hero both of the comick and tragick part, is a young man of great abilities and violent passions, whose sentiments are right, though his actions are wrong; whose virtues are obscured by negligence, and whose understanding is dissipated by levity. In his idle hours he is rather loose than wicked, and when the occasion forces out his latent qualities, he is great without effort, and brave without tumult. The trifler is roused into a hero, and the hero again reposes into the trifle. The character is great, original and just.

> —*Samuel Johnson*, The Plays of William Shakespeare, 1785

Very conscious of the way that men respond to the image of royalty, and no less instinctive a politician than his father, Hal is the creator as well as the creature of political mythology, the author as well as the hero of his legend.

> —*Robert Ornstein*, A Kingdom for a Stage, 1972

On Falstaff

[At Gad's Hill] What he leaves behind is not jeering contempt for a butt or a coward, but affection; an affection compounded of many simples: laughing sympathy for one who has "more flesh than another man, and therefore more frailty", astonishment at the quick dexterity with which he nevertheless carries his guts away, merriment at the turning of the tables upon him, delight in the sheer absurdity of his predicament, and above all—quite illogically, though inextricably—blended with the rest, gratitude to the player for the cleverness of the whole entertainment.

—*John Dover Wilson*, The
Fortunes of Falstaff, *1943*

On Hotspur

Hotspur's speech [Act I, Scene iii, lines 30-71], by far the most sustained in the play to this point, is so full of detail, so quick and apparently spontaneous in elaboration, . . . so varied by impersonations of the "popinjay", and yet so strong and lively in rhythm that his character is strongly established in its own right by this one manifestation. The speech glistens with light and shade and is charged with energy. Given the active performance implied by the language, Hotspur usurps all attention.

—*John Russell Brown*, Shakespeare
in Performance, *1976*

On the Meaning of the Play

Analysis leaves us then, with symbols of Power and Appetite as the keys to the play's meaning: Power and Appetite, the two sides of Commodity . . . Those who see the world of *Henry IV* as some vital, joyous Renaissance England must go behind the facts Shakespeare presents. It is a world where to be normal is to be anti-social, and to be social is to be anti-human. Humanity is split in two. One half is banished to an underworld where dignity and decency must inevitably submerge in brutality and riot. The other half is restricted to an overworld where the same dignity and decency succumb to heartlessness and frigidity.

—*John F. Dandy*, Shakespeare's
Doctrine of Nature, *1949*

NOTES